OUTCAST

OUTCAST

How Jews Were Banished from
the Anti-Racist Imagination

CAMILA BASSI

First published in 2023 by No Pasaran Media

Copyright © Camila Bassi 2023

The moral right of Camila Bassi to be identified as the author of this work has been asserted in accordance with the Copyright, Designs and Patents Act 1988. All rights reserved. No part of this publication may be reproduced or transmitted in any form or by any means, electronic or mechanical including photocopying, recording or any information storage or retrieval system, without prior permission in writing from the publishers.

ISBN 9781915036780

Also available as an ebook
ISBN 9781915036797

Typeset by seagulls.net
Cover design by Emma Ewbank
Image on p.149 from Lebrecht Music & Arts / Alamy Stock Photo
Project management by whitefox
Printed and bound by CPI Books Ltd

Camila Bassi is a human geography academic whose principal research interests are the geographies of 'race', ethnicity and sexuality, and Marxist geographies. She has been a political activist on the British Left since 1996 and has published on a wide range of social and political issues. Her blog, *Anaemic On A Bike*, contains posts which synthesise her academic ideas with wider political currents.

For Darshan and Zubin

CONTENTS

Foreword by Lesley Klaff   xi

Introduction   1

Chapter 1   Racism and the Left's 'Jewish Question'   5

Chapter 2   Racism Beyond the Colour Line   29

Chapter 3   The Academic Left's 'Jewish Question' and Colonial Model of Racism   67

Chapter 4   Escaping the Impasse of the 'Zionist Other'   99

Chapter 5   Building an Alliance for Human Liberation   137

Chapter 6   Conclusion   151

Acknowledgements   161

References   163

Index   176

FOREWORD

There are many reasons why *Outcast* is an exceptionally illuminating book, not least because it answers questions which have perplexed Jews and researchers on antisemitism for quite some time: Why does the 'anti-racist Left' fail to see Jews as victims of racism in the same way that it sees people of colour as victims of racism? Why does it treat claims of antisemitism with contempt? Why does the anti-racist Left only approve of those 'exceptional' Jews who are prepared to distance themselves from Israel and Zionism and renounce the Jewish right to national self-determination while upholding that right for others, including the Palestinians? Why does the anti-racist Left regard Israel as a uniquely illegitimate state which must be eliminated, and Zionism as a particularly deplorable racism, rather than as a nationalist response to anti-Jewish persecution?

The author, Dr Camila Bassi, not only explains and answers these questions but, in so doing, she exposes the contemporary manifestations of anti-Jewish racism on the anti-racist Left that are consistently denied. Dr Bassi, moreover, provides her exposé from the unique perspective of an 'insider': she is a member of the anti-racist Left herself, being a comrade in the Alliance for Workers' Liberty (AWL) and serving as the Chair of the Sheffield Hallam University branch of the UCU for many years. It is this 'insider' perspective that sets *Outcast* apart from much of the other literature on contemporary Left antisemitism, which is written from the perspective of the outsider looking in. Dr Bassi's 'insider' status also allows her to issue a powerful plea to her comrades on the anti-racist Left to recognise their own entrapment in 'the Jewish question', the anti-Jewish racism that creates it, and to abandon it in favour of realising a vision filled with co-existence for all. To do otherwise, she advises them, is not only a betrayal of the Jews, but also a tragic betrayal of the Left's universal and democratic values.

Of particular interest to those concerned with contemporary Left antisemitism are several insightful and honest critiques of the academic and activist Left's attitude to Jews, Israel, and Zionism. For example, *Outcast* critiques the Left's preferred definition of antisemitism as 'hostility to Jews qua Jews', showing that it fails to take account of the racialisation that is central to all racisms. *Outcast*'s critique of identity politics, and its associated 'cultural essentialism', is as refreshing as it is illuminating. Bassi details the negative application of identity politics to Jews to essentialise them as 'the enemy within the nation state', and to Israel to exceptionalise it as 'the enemy nation state'. This clearly illustrates the continuum between classic antisemitism and contemporary Left anti-Zionism. *Outcast*'s critique of the colonial model of racism which, Dr Bassi convincingly argues, constructs Jews as 'uber white' and 'privileged' and Zionism as 'racism', and frames Palestinian suicide bombers as part of the anti-racist struggle, is very instructive. This is especially so given the current trend in academia to regard 'race' and 'racism' as only possible along the colour-line. *Outcast* is brutally frank about the Left's abusive use of the apartheid and Nazi analogies and settler-colonial paradigm which, Dr Bassi convincingly argues, are used tactically to galvanise international support for a one-state solution post Oslo.

But *Outcast* offers hope and salvation with its discussion of a Marxist tradition that is free of 'the Jewish question'. Dr Bassi draws on the work of key Marxists such as the late sociologist Maxime Rodinson to offer an assessment of Zionism in the context of European antisemitism, recognising it as a response to anti-Jewish persecution. She also reveals, in the light of the recognition by Marx, Lenin and Trotsky of the right to national self-determination for all peoples including the Jews, that it is the duty of socialists to defend the basic democratic right of the Jewish people, as well as the Palestinian people, to their own state. *Outcast* also very helpfully discusses the work on black antisemitism of American intellectuals Cornel West and Henry Louis Gates, Jr., who recognise that anti-Jewish racism is the bedfellow of anti-black racism. Dr Bassi offers this work as a discussion point for those on the anti-racist Left who respond with acceptance to allegations of anti-black racism but who dismiss Jewish complaints of antisemitism as a cover for 'racist Israel'.

Such is the passion and conviction with which *Outcast* is written that one might readily assume that Dr Camila Bassi is Jewish or is strongly Zionist. In fact, she is neither. She is a British Indian who grew up in the Sikh and Hindu cultures and she is not especially pro-Zionist. The book makes clear that she believes that the tragedy of 1948 was that one national group, the Jews, realised its right to national self-determination at the expense of another national group, the Palestinians. She also accepts the view that there are racist and colonial dimensions to Israel, and that the policies and actions of the Israeli state towards the Palestinians are 'despicable'. Nevertheless, Dr Bassi recognises that the only way forward is for the anti-racist Left to understand that there is nothing *exceptional* about Israel or Zionism, to support a two-state solution to the Israeli-Palestinian conflict, and to abandon its 'culture war' against pro-Zionist Jews. In this exceptionally insightful book, Dr Bassi accordingly calls on the activist and academic Left to open up spaces for discussion and debate on these issues. We should all – Jews, the Left, and everyone else concerned about these matters – profoundly hope that they agree to do so.

Lesley Klaff, Editor-in-Chief, *Journal of Contemporary Antisemitism*

INTRODUCTION

'Society, confronted with political, economic, and legal equality for Jews, made it quite clear that none of its classes was prepared to grant them social equality, and that only exceptions from the Jewish people would be received. Jews who heard the strange compliment that they were exceptions, exceptional Jews, knew quite well that it was this very ambiguity – that they were Jews and yet presumably not *like* Jews – which opened the doors of society to them. If they desired this kind of intercourse, they tried, therefore, "to be and yet not to be Jews". The seeming paradox had a solid basis in fact. What non-Jewish society demanded was that the newcomer be as "educated" as itself, and that, although he [*sic*] not behave like an "ordinary Jew", he be and produce something out of the ordinary, since, after all, he was a Jew.' (Arendt, 1976: 56)

As a British Indian who grew up among Sikh and Hindu cultures, the Left does not expect me to be exceptional. No member of my family is required to publicly display our disapproval of the hegemonic forces of anti-Muslim racism in India or anti-Muslim racism prevalent in the Indian diaspora. No descendants of my past extended family, who were victims and participants of violence during the 1947 Partition of India, are obliged to express that they have learnt a lesson and are now model citizens of the world. My ethnic identity as British Indian is left alone.

By contrast, those who identify as Jewish are not left alone. Instead, the Left demands the exceptional Jew. I find the leftist ultimatum placed on Israeli and diasporic Jews extraordinary. Ordinary Jewish people are required to deny the existence of anti-Jewish racism on the Left while demonstrating that they subscribe to a resolution to the Palestinian-Israeli conflict that erases the nation state of Israel proper (i.e., on pre-1967 borders, prior to the occupation of the West Bank and Gaza Strip). Furthermore, Jewish people must show that, as descendants of the victims of the Holocaust, they know better than anyone else not to become the persecutors. In short, Jewish people are either doomed as ordinary Jews or salvaged as exceptional Jews.

This situation is one aspect of a wider phenomenon in which the recognition of antisemitism in early-to-present racist thought (which I also refer to as anti-Jewish racism) has been banished from the contemporary anti-racist imagination and struggle. Instead of recognition, what one finds is contempt, proclaimed by many leftists, at the very suggestion of anti-Jewish racism in their ideas and ranks. A sense of moral superiority drives a refusal to even see the accuser of anti-Jewish racism as worthy of consideration. And yet, no other claim of any other kind of racism provokes such disdain and dismissal. How have Jews who raise the issue of antisemitism on the Left been cast out by otherwise committed anti-racists? The answer lies in the retorted cry to the cry of 'antisemitism!', 'Zionism!', that is, in the vilification of Jewish nationalism as an especially deplorable racism and colonialism.

Outcast is an exposition of how the anti-racist imagination fails to see Jewish people as victims of racism because the Left damns ordinary Jews, who are in any way associated with Zionism and Israel, as its racist pariahs. This, I argue, is a product of an academic framework that reduces the study of racism to its colonial moment (and as 'what white people think and do to black and brown people') and of 'the Jewish question': that is, the racist idea that something must be done to redress the harm which Jews inflict on humanity. Together this has led to the categorisation of Zionism, Israel and all related Jews as a Jewish collective body with an intrinsic disposition to racist repression.

In Chapter Two, I discuss how academic enquiry into racism since the 1960s has tended towards understanding racism exclusively in relation to colonialism and as a 'white over black' structural relationship, with the consequence that Zionism has been conceived in exclusive racist terms and antisemitism has disappeared from view. Drawing primarily on the scholarship of Robert Miles and George Mosse, I offer an alternative and wider history of racism and its relationship (in addition to colonialism) to capitalism and nationalism, and a trajectory therein of past-to-present anti-Jewish racism.

Chapter Three reveals that when a colonial model of racism and 'the Jewish question' merge into an understanding of the Palestinian-Israeli conflict, Zionism and all associated Jews become the representation of racism incarnate demanding the unparalleled elimination of Israel. Specifically, I lay bare a body of contemporary academic literature, with origins in the New Left of the late 1960s and 1970s, which identifies Zionism and Israel as a particularly harmful settler-colonialism, a particularly harmful ethnic cleansing, a particularly harmful and illegitimate nationalism, and a particularly harmful racism, and that positions Palestinian Islamist resistance as – at best, misguided – anti-colonialist and anti-racist struggle.

In response, in Chapter Four, I resuscitate a Marxist tradition to the Jewish collective and the Palestinian-Israeli conflict that is free from 'the Jewish question', and which takes into account the historical context of European antisemitism, colonialism and nationalism. Notably, I excavate the work of the late independent Marxist scholar, Maxime Rodinson, as an exemplar of how the racist and colonial dimensions of Israel can be comprehended relatively, without an absolute moral damnation of the Jewish collective or moralistic resolve to destroy Israel.

Recognising our 'overwhelming sameness' (Gilroy, 2000: 29), in Chapter Five I look outwards to reflect on how currents of the Left, by essentialising 'race' (i.e., by giving socially constructed difference a natural essence and reality), have positioned themselves on the wrong side of history in the fight for human liberation. I present the writings of Cornel West and Henry Louis Gates, Jr. on black antisemitism as an opening for discussion with a Left that regards itself as a vanguard in the fight against anti-black racism while dismissing anti-Jewish racism in its ideological midst.

In sum, *Outcast* is an endeavour for solidarity that escapes the restrictions of 'race' and other politicised identities, which divide and exclude us, and instead calls for a genuinely universal alliance for political and human emancipation.

Chapter 1

RACISM AND THE LEFT'S 'JEWISH QUESTION'

The story of Balbir Singh Sodhi, the first fatal victim of post-9/11 anti-Muslim racism in the United States, offers an important lesson on the nature of racism more generally. Leaving India during the late 1980s, amid anti-Sikh pogroms that followed the assassination of Prime Minister Indira Gandhi, Sodhi resettled in California, working at a 7-Eleven and as a taxi driver, prior to running a gas station in Mesa, Arizona. He was shot and murdered at his place of work on 15 September 2001. His perpetrator had stated his intention to 'go out and shoot some towel-heads'; apt then is the bronze plaque memorial for Sodhi, which reads: 'He was killed simply because of the way he looked' (cited in Kaur, 2021).

However, it is a partial explanation only that Sodhi, a practising Sikh man, was murdered because his turban and beard misidentified him as a Muslim. Racism is an ideological representation of the world that categorises and ascribes meaning to 'Them/the Other' and 'Us/the Self' based on *the idea of 'race'*. This process of representing meaning, vis-à-vis the idea of 'race', is racialisation. Furthermore, racism begets a struggle between the racialised Other who is deemed a threat to the racialised Self. Racialisation is a false attribution of meaning to socially constructed groups of people based on the essentialist idea that the universal collective of human beings is divisible into distinct categories of 'race' characterised by biologically or culturally innate differences.

As such, Balbir Singh Sodhi was a fatal victim of anti-Muslim racism because he was *racialised* as the harmful Other: the turbaned

Islamic terrorist or 'towel-head'. Moreover, because racism is *always* a mistaken identification of human beings, one does not need to identify as a Muslim to be a victim of anti-Muslim racism, since it is the racist who decides who is and who isn't the Muslim Other.

The common retort against allegations of anti-Jewish racism on the Left is the use of a definition of antisemitism by the academic Brian Klug (2013: 3): 'antisemitism is hostility to Jews *as* Jews (or *because* they are Jews)'. So the defence goes, 'we are not antisemitic because we are not hostile to Jews as Jews'. A fundamental problem with this definition is that it misses the racialisation which is central to all racism: the process of categorising and giving meaning to ethnic and/or phenotypical difference as natural 'racial' difference that defines the racialised Self vis-à-vis the racialised Other. A definition of anti-Muslim racism as hostility to Muslims as Muslims, or anti-Jewish racism as hostility to Jews as Jews, offers no explanatory power to the process of racialisation that creates the very *idea* of *Muslim* or *Jew* in 'Muslims as Muslims' or 'Jews as Jews'. Simply put, to comprehend racism fully, we need to escape the idea that 'races' have meaningful intrinsic traits and instead recognise that 'racial' categories are social constructs, positive or negative, which have been created and normalised in society.

Central to racism then is the idea of 'race', which, in the case of anti-Jewish racism on the Left presents in the idea of 'the Jewish question' – 'the classic term for the representation of Jews as harmful to humanity as a whole' – and therein the oppositional racialisation of the exceptional Jew and the ordinary Jew (Fine and Spencer, 2017: 2). As the academics Robert Fine and Philip Spencer (2017) explain, in their book *Antisemitism and the left: On the return of the Jewish question*, 'the Jewish question' is to antisemitism what sociologist Paul Gilroy terms raciology (i.e., the idea of 'race') is to racism more generally. On the problem of raciology, Gilroy (2000: 29) suggests:

'Whether it is articulated in the more specialized tongues of biological science and pseudo-science or in a vernacular idiom of culture and common sense, the term "race" conjures up a peculiarly resistant variety of natural difference. It stands outside of, and in opposition to, most attempts to render it secondary to the overwhelming sameness that overdetermines social relationships between people and continually betrays the tragic predicaments of their common species life. The undervalued power of this crushingly obvious, almost banal human sameness, so close and basically invariant that it regularly passes unremarked upon, also confirms that the crisis of raciological reasoning presents an important opportunity where it points toward the possibility of leaving "race" behind, of setting aside its disabling use as we move out of the time in which it could have been expected to make sense.'

In other words, the anti-racist imagination needs to escape the idea of 'race' because this very idea functions to 'estrange' human beings from one another and 'amputate' our 'common humanity' (Gilroy, 2000: 15). Similarly, the anti-racist imagination must escape the idea of 'the Jewish question', that is, the question of what is to be done with the Jews who are harmful to humanity, since this question tears 'apart the universal, particular and singular aspects of the human condition' and situates the Left against those whom it signifies as ordinary Jews (Fine and Spencer, 2017: 3). The contemporary Left's vision of universalism and common humanity has so far failed to escape 'the Jewish question', including the demand that ordinary Jews must become exceptional Jews, specifically, that they must become comrades in the mission to absolutely defeat and erase the Jewish nation state and its blemish on humanity.

THE LEFT'S IDENTITY SCRIPT FOR 'THE JEWS'

The identity politics of the Left is an opposition to the identity politics of the Right. The problem with identity politics per se is that it is based on cultural essentialism. Cultural essentialism is the assumption that our cultural differences are decisive and the expression of different inner realities; as such it denies our sameness and potential for governing together as a universal collective. The sociologist Avtar Brah (1996: 92) usefully points out that it is possible to acknowledge 'the historical specificity' of particular cultural formations, along with recognising our universal commonality that comes from 'historically variable' and constantly changing experience, without recourse to cultural essentialism. She calls for a focus on communities in struggle rather than identity politics, and to conceive of cultures 'less' as concrete things and 'more as processes' (ibid: 92). The danger of cultural essentialism on the Left is that it effectively takes the cultural essentialism of the political Right into the struggle for liberation, and in doing so it leaves the door open to the very oppressive ideas and ideologies one is attempting to resist. Moreover, cultural essentialism on the Left fixes people to their designated cultural differences, instead of understanding that we are constantly an outcome of societal processes that construct such differences and that we are also an agent in these processes which define us as 'white', 'black', 'Jewish', and so on.

'Race', like other socially constructed differences, does not reflect a material inner nature, but is an idea of difference borne from the material relations of society that has reality for us in society. When anti-racists contest negative racist ideas about 'race' at the same time as mobilising 'racial' identities in their anti-racist struggle, the goal of human liberation is self-defeated, because, as the sociologist Robert Miles makes plain: 'the strategy that wholeheartedly grounds itself in a discourse that continues to give legitimacy to the notion that there are such things as "races"' is 'handing a card to the racists' (cited in Ashe and McGeever, 2011: 2024).

If the Left was free from cultural essentialism, then 'ordinary Jews' would not be damned unless they could prove themselves 'extraordinary Jews', and Zionism would not be condemned as an *unprecedented* aberration and barrier to humanity's progress. Anti-Jewish racism on the Left makes monsters out of human beings. The Zionist monster looms large on a global stage, with expansive tentacles. This monster is the Other to the politicised identity of the anti-racist, anti-colonialist, anti-imperialist, and anti-capitalist Self, whose mission is to rescue not just Palestinian victims but all victims of Zionism, which is anyone who dares to speak the truth about Israel. The Left's identity script for 'the Jews' and 'the Palestinians' in the tragic drama of the Palestinian-Israeli conflict freezes the conflict in time – both are passive actors, not active agents: the Israeli Jew is so thoroughly subsumed in racism and colonial aggression that they are a lost cause to the Left; the Palestinian suicide bomber is either a fictive racist character to mask the real racism of Israel or the product of Israeli Jewish racist repression who is left with no other choice.

Anti-Jewish racism on the Left makes the Palestinian-Israeli conflict indistinguishable from the idea of the harmful Jew, who is the essence of imperialism and capitalism. Yet, as Marx (1965: 14) reminds us, our comprehension of the world does not start with humans 'as narrated, thought of, imagined, conceived' to arrive at humans 'in the flesh', nor should it assume that humans are merely the products of material reality. History is an ever-changing outcome of the conflicts between human wills and conditions of existence, as Engels (1998: 71–72) states:

'We make history ourselves, but first of all, under very definite assumptions and conditions. [...] history is made in such a way that the final result always arises from conflicts between individual wills, of which each in turn has been made what it is by a variety of particular conditions of life. Thus, there are innumerable criss-crossing forces, an infinite series of parallelograms of forces'.

All people, including Jewish people, have human agency and are constantly subject to change. The Left which has forgotten this is a Left that has lost its political compass.

The limitation of all forms of essentialist identity politics is that this politics does not reach out in an on-going search for our sameness amid our differences, because it removes us from realising the ideal of a universal alliance of human beings. Worse still, 'current forms of identity politics become attached to destructive modes of their own subjection' (Cadman, 2006: 140) because politicised identities emerging out of capitalist social relations, 'insofar as they are premised on exclusion from a universal ideal, require that ideal, as well as their exclusion from it, for their own continuing existence as identities' (Brown, 1995: 65). In simple terms, in the context of the Palestinian-Israeli conflict, politicised identities of the Self based on the Zionist Other, require this enemy to stay put.

THE LEFT'S GOOD JEWS AND BAD JEWS

A definition of antisemitism as hostility to Jews as Jews makes it possible to boldly assert that criticism of Israel is not antisemitic, thus failing to see that, while criticism of Israel is not per se antisemitic, there is a real potential for anti-Israeli sentiment to descend into anti-Jewish racism (in which Jewish people are essentialised as 'bad Jews' or 'good Jews').

The definitive claim commonly made on the Left that 'anti-Zionism is not antisemitism' is effectively based on a process of racialisation. This contention is illustrated by the Israeli academic Neve Gordon in his 2018 *London Review of Books* article 'The "New

Anti-Semitism"'. Gordon's (2018) argument, which rejects the notion of a new or left antisemitism, hinges on his preference for a definition of antisemitism 'as hatred of Jews per se' (akin to, hostility to Jews as Jews). 'Many Jews are not Zionists', Gordon (2018) states. In other words, many Jews are not ordinary Jews but exceptional Jews. Traditionally, he continues, 'to call someone "anti-Semitic" is to expose and condemn their racism; in the new case, the charge "anti-Semite" is used to defend racism', as such, 'it is possible to be both a Zionist and an anti-Semite'.

What Gordon is presenting here is actually an oppositional racialisation of the good Jew, who has broken with Zionism, and its Other, the bad Jew, who weaponises antisemitism as a facade for the racist Zionist state. Gordon (2018) negates the notion of new or left antisemitism by relegating antisemitism to the past and by positioning those who claim there is antisemitism on the Left as those who 'seek to legitimate the discrimination against and subjugation of Palestinians': the Jew who manufactures racism to conceal actual racist ideas and practice. Terming all Jews who raise a complaint of antisemitism as weaponisers of antisemitism and propagandists for an expansionist Israel is a racialisation of ordinary Jews, with the requirement to prove themselves otherwise: exceptional Jews.

There are many on the Left who see antisemitism as a fabricated product of the Israeli state designed to shut down criticism of Israel, and/or as a real and understandable by-product of Israeli state and military violence against Palestinians, and/or as a phenomenon of the far Right only; subsequently, they shut down the space to consider how the racialisation of Jewish people manifests itself ideologically on the Left. Calling out the weaponisation of antisemitism by a right-wing Israeli government and defending one's right to condemn the Israeli state's oppression of the Palestinians should not then impede recognition of the presence of anti-Jewish racism in much leftist criticism of Israel.

While Klug's definition of antisemitism is actually more sophisticated than its frequent application on the Left as 'hostility to Jews as Jews', since he understands a process of projection leading to hostility to Jews, Klug (2013: 5) nevertheless holds on to the idea of the good Jew:

> 'antisemitism is a form of hostility to Jews as Jews, where Jews are perceived as something other than what they are. Or more succinctly: hostility to Jews as *not* Jews. […] For, even if some real Jews fit the stereotype, the "Jew" towards whom the antisemite feels hostile is not a *real* Jew at all: the figure of the "Jew" is a frozen image projected onto the screen of a living person.'

Hostility to 'Jews as *Jews*' is a co-constructed racialisation that includes '*Jews* as Jews' – both 'Jews' require examination and deconstruction. In Klug's definition, the necessary analytical work of thinking through what the Left means by Jews in either instance is bypassed. Should this work be done, what could be called into question is both the idea of the pro-Zionist regressive Jew and the anti-Zionist progressive Jew. In other words, the defence against the allegation of anti-Jewish racism that one is not hostile to Jews as Jews holds up the good Jew, which itself is part of the problem.

DAPHNE AND 'THE JEWISH QUESTION'

A rare moment where the space to consider anti-Jewish racism on the Left was not shut down was Klug's intervention in a Socialist Workers' Party (SWP) Marxism Festival public meeting (SWP TV, 2017). His credentials, which undoubtedly earned him the invite, were noted at the start: his benchmark understanding of antisemitism as hostility to Jews as Jews. Nevertheless, Klug calls into question: 'a discourse [on the Left] that folds Zionism [i.e., Jewish nationalism] completely, without remainder, into the history of European imperialism and colonialism, as if Zionism does not have its roots in the Jewish experience […] of centuries of exclusion and persecution in Europe' (Klug in SWP TV, 2017).

He tells the story of Daphne, a Jewish anti-Zionist and socialist, who proposed a motion at her constituency Labour party meeting criticising Ken Livingstone's comments linking Zionism with Nazism:

> 'I quote her, "everyone who spoke against the motion suggested that it was part of a plot by Israel or that it was an attempt to prevent discussion of Israel". Daphne was made to feel, in her own words, "an agent of the Israeli state". Her opponents didn't address her arguments, they didn't try to defend what he [Livingstone] said, Daphne told me, "they were", I quote, "only interested in discrediting those behind the motion by linking it to Israel or right-wing manoeuvring in the Party". In effect, her opponents, I quote, "shut down discussion, I felt I was being silenced", she said.' (Klug in SWP TV, 2017)

Klug concludes this story as one of 'an injustice':

> 'All too often, when a Jewish person, even an anti-Zionist, anti-occupation Jew, says they feel uncomfortable or worse with the way in which Jews or Israel are spoken about, the knee-jerk reaction is to scoff and to cry "Zionism!", we wouldn't treat members of other racialised minorities this way, then why the Jews?' (Klug in SWP TV, 2017)

But this is not simply 'an injustice'. Instead, what the case of Daphne reveals is an exceptionalisation of Zionism and Israel, and therein an essentialisation of Jewish people. Daphne, like all people who identify as Jewish, is tied to 'the Jewish question': Jews are compelled to prove themselves other than the bad Jew. Klug's narration of the story of

Daphne as an injustice pivots on her being a lifelong anti-Zionist and socialist Jew, that is, a 'good Jew': he reasons, even when people should know better than to think Daphne is an agent of the Israeli state, they still accuse her of being an agent of the Israeli state, and fail to take her experience of antisemitism seriously. For Klug, part of his frustration, it seems, is that Daphne should be recognised as an exceptional Jew but is mistakenly viewed as an ordinary Jew.

From the floor of the meeting, the academic Jonathan Rosenhead (chairman of the British Committee for the Universities of Palestine) derides Daphne: 'We are not obliged to be hypersensitive about people who are still feeling offended that Israel can be criticised in serious ways' (Rosenhead in SWP TV, 2017).

The SWP position more generally consisted of three interlinked elements: the threat of antisemitism comes from the far Right; the SWP are the true opponents of fascism, racism and antisemitism, not the Zionists, who capitulate to antisemitism and promote an illegitimate, racist colonial state; and, the SWP must engage with Jewish students on university campuses who are attracted to soft Zionism to get them to break from Zionism (SWP TV, 2017). This last element shows again the requisite placed on Jews to become something exceptional.

THE ACADEMIC LEFT'S BLIND SPOT
AND LITMUS TEST FOR JEWS

I work as an academic in the British higher education system. On our university campuses, we teach a significant body of international students from China, some of whom are loyal to the Chinese Communist Party and some of whom are not. Left academics have shown no inclination to call on Chinese student societies to publicly state their opposition to the Chinese state's mass detention of Uyghur Muslims in Xinjiang or its repression of pro-democracy movements inside China and in Hong Kong, even when, on our doorstep, pro-democracy students from Hong Kong face off against pro-Chinese Communist Party, student counter-protests (Drury, 2019).

By contrast, student members of the Union of Jewish Students are both called upon and called out as complicit agents of an especially oppressive and illegitimate racist state. A motion passed at my local University and Colleges Union (UCU) branch in November 2021, in defence of the academic David Miller, who was sacked by his employer, the University of Bristol, after complaints of antisemitism, stated that his naming of 'a student organisation [i.e., Bristol's Jewish Society of the Union of Jewish Students] as acting in the interests of a foreign state, Israel' does not 'constitute antisemitism' (UCU Hallam, 2021). I met with the President of my local Jewish Society after the motion was passed, and felt deep shame as she, in an effort to overcome the bind that her lecturers had placed on her, explained her day-to-day activities as President, which did not, she spelt out, include being on the payroll of the Israeli government and acting as its mouthpiece.

The deteriorating political position that my national union, UCU, has taken on the question of anti-Jewish racism (in a series of motions passed at its annual delegates congress) illustrates a blind spot pervasive on the academic Left: in 2006, rejecting the notion that 'criticism of the Israeli government is in itself anti-Semitic' and asserting that 'defenders of the Israeli government's actions have used a charge of anti-Semitism as a tactic in order to smother democratic debate and in the context of Higher Education to restrict academic freedom'; in 2007, that 'criticism of Israel cannot be construed as anti-Semitic'; and in 2008, that 'criticisms of Israel or Israeli policy are not, as such, anti-Semitic' (cited in Fine and Spencer, 2017: 119).

The denial by UCU in 2007 that criticism of Israel can sometimes be antisemitic is a singular blind spot. There is no intellectual consistency here, since any academic who subscribes to the view that criticism of Israel is never antisemitic must logically draw the conclusion that criticism of any country, including on the continents of Latin

America, Africa or Asia, is never racist, but of course such a conclusion is not drawn. It is, in fact, the UCU position that the allegation of antisemitism is cover for Zionism. As a consequence, this trade union, in its general opposition to racism, omits anti-Jewish racism in its desire to denounce Israel. It is perfectly possible for academics to criticise the Israeli state's ongoing repression of the Palestinians without being antisemitic. Anti-Jewish racism enters this critical space when Israel is irrationally and moralistically deemed the most harmful, deplorable and illegitimate nation state that must accordingly be destroyed, and when Jews who are associated with this nation state are singled out for a litmus test: prove yourself an exceptional Jew or remain damned.

UCU has also advocated for an academic boycott of Israel, thus enacting its litmus test for Jews, which is demanded of no other working class worldwide. I spoke on this debate at the UCU national congress in 2009, arguing for working class solidarity across borders rather than a boycott that effectively writes off the Israeli working class by conflating it with the ruling class in Israel (Hirsh, 2018; Shepherd, 2009).

The case of the left-wing Israeli academic Oren Yiftachel is revealing here. Yiftachel submitted a co-authored paper to the international journal *Political Geography* in April 2002. The editor who received it, David Slater, returned the paper unopened, with a note that he, as a signatory of a letter calling for a boycott of Israeli academics, would not be accepting the paper for review. In the *Guardian*, Slater stated that he was 'not sure to what extent he [Yiftachel] had been critical of Israel' (cited in Beckett, 2002). In fact, given the paper was unread, Yiftachel failed the litmus test simply because he was an Israeli Jew. By January 2003, amid mounting publicity, Slater professed an error of judgement and sent the paper to reviewers, and, after revisions, it was published in 2004 (Beckett, 2002; O'Loughlin, 2004). Yiftachel's paper, co-authored with the Palestinian academic, As'ad Ghanem, was a comparative analysis of ethnocratic regimes including Israel (see: Yiftachel and Ghanem, 2004). In a series of articles reflecting back on this case, published in *Political Geography*, Slater (2004: 646) declares his support 'even more strongly now' for an academic boycott of Israel, but of institutions, not individuals.

Any notion that an academic boycott of Israel might blend into anti-Jewish racism is, moreover, dismissed by those who support the wider Boycott, Divestment and Sanctions campaign. As David Storey (2005: 995) asserts:

'While some argue that attempts to boycott Israel are anti-Semitic, it should be pretty obvious that such arguments are pernicious and serve to nullify criticism in a way analogous to the invoking of anti-Americanism in attempts to disarm those critical of US foreign policy. While not denying the disturbing evidence of anti-Semitism, it should be clear that criticism of the actions of a state and its government is not the same as racism.'

Implicit here is the charge that the claimants, the 'bad Jews', defend the indefensible by cloaking racism with fabricated claims of antisemitism.

Genuinely comparative criticism of the nation state of Israel and its government is different from the exceptionalising of the nation state of Israel as a problematically *Jewish* state that requires dismantlement, and the decision, through an academic boycott of Israel, to include a relatively left-of-society academic working class within its ruling class. Stanley Waterman (2004: 999) remarks on the case of Yiftachel, 'it seems that there aren't any other states in the world worthy of boycotting except a Jewish one', concluding that 'some British academics and intellectuals are so imbued with post-colonialist guilt that they fail to see where they fit into the wider geopolitical picture' (ibid: 1000). Waterman is too generous here to assume naivety on the part of those endorsing an academic boycott of Israel.

The thrust of academic literature published on the Palestinian-Israeli conflict, especially in more recent years, regards any resolution to the conflict that does not undo the nation state of Israel as unacceptable.

THE LEFT'S PUBLIC INTELLECTUALS AND EXCEPTIONAL JEWS

The conclusion made in academic work that the Jewish nation state must cease to exist, which I expound upon in Chapter Three, gives the activist Left an intellectual legitimacy to go further than simply denying the existence of anti-Jewish racism within its ranks. Implicating the Jewish Other as part and parcel of a clandestine and sinister global Zionist network to shut down criticism of Israel, dominate the world and threaten world peace, it is demanded that this Jewish Other stop being a Zionist Jew to belong in the commune of humanity. Furthermore, this activist Left milieu has its academics-cum-public intellectuals who appear or are cited to speak the truth on Israel.

In this section, I analyse some of the public talks given by three such individuals: former associate professor Norman Finkelstein (author of *The Holocaust Industry*; *Image and Reality of the Israel-Palestine Conflict* and *Gaza*), professor Ilan Pappé (whose books include, *The Ethnic Cleansing of Palestine*; *Ten Myths About Israel* and *The Biggest Prison on Earth*) and the sacked professor David Miller (co-author of *Bad News for Labour: Antisemitism, the Party and Public Belief*).

Finkelstein (2015), in an address to the Philosophy Society at University College Dublin, responds to a question on whether there is a rise of antisemitism in Europe by stating: 'there's just no evidence for these claims about a rise of antisemitism in Europe and we have to all renew our battle against antisemitism, it's just not true.' He elaborates:

'By far and away the most accepted minority in all the western countries, by far and away, are Jews [...] the sign of acceptance, when you know what's called assimilation has tipped, the sign is always inter-marriage [...] Well, in the United States today, I would say, there isn't a single ruling class family that hasn't inter-married with Jews.' (Finkelstein, 2015)

Finkelstein (2015) goes on to qualify his answer:

'What you do find is, if you look at the opinion polls, there is a spike in antisemitism [...] every time Israel launches one of its murderous invasions [...] That's not antisemitism in any meaningful sense, that's a state that calls itself Jewish carrying out in a horrifying way and so people react to it against Jews, if you want to prevent antisemitism there's two things you can do, number one you can stop committing massacres and number two stop calling yourself a Jewish state, just call yourself Israel, and then I think the number of antisemitic acts will go back down.'

He concludes:

'If you had a choice, in any European country where they say "oh the antisemitism is going berserk" [...] if you're in France, would you rather be Jewish or short, would you rather be Jewish or obese [...] would you rather be Jewish or ugly [...] the world is so plagued by so many horrifying crimes, so much suffering [...] so okay some people have some prejudices about me, but if you take it at the legal level, Jews are doing better than anybody else, so all this talk of antisemitism, it's just a joke.' (Finkelstein, 2015)

Finkelstein (2015) negates the reality of antisemitism by trivialising it and arguing that what might be considered antisemitism is not actually antisemitism but rather an understandable response (i.e., blowback) to the murderous actions of Israel, so when Israel rightly ceases to be a Jewish nation state, the so-called problem of antisemitism will disappear. Under the guise of a point about Jewish assimilation (assimilation being acculturation to a general population, which is not what Finkelstein means here), he contends that antisemitism does not exist because Jews are incorporated into the ruling class: again, 'there isn't a single ruling class family that hasn't intermarried with Jews' (ibid). In sum, Finkelstein (2015) asserts, in response to a question about antisemitism, that antisemitism is a joke; Jews cause antisemitism; Jews are particularly powerful; and, Israel should cease being Jewish. Accordingly, he banishes antisemitism from the anti-racist imagination by presenting 'the Jewish question': Jews are not harmed, they are harmful.

In a public meeting hosted by the Socialist Workers' Party, titled 'Anti-Zionism is not antisemitism', Pappé (2019) lays bare the relationship between anti-Zionism, Zionism and the allegations of antisemitism in the Labour party under Jeremy Corbyn's leadership. Pappé (2019) explains:

'The inability to cover the criminality in Gaza is one of the reasons that you get instead a hyper inflated coverage of a few emails that may or may not be antisemitic, as if this is an issue that threatens people's life or existence, and this imbalance between a manipulated hysteria of something that doesn't happen and a total ignorance of what really happens is one of the major challenges that this ridiculous equation of antisemitism with anti-Zionism is causing, and which we will have to challenge.'

On the journalists who covered the antisemitism allegations in the Labour party, he speculates:

'Either these people are intelligent and I suppose many people who work in *The Times* and BBC and so on are intelligent and that's worse, that means they know exactly what they are doing, because they're afraid, because someone is paying them, I don't know, I don't know, I'm not going to investigate, I'm interested in the outcome not in their motives [...] or [...] they're ignorant [...] on an area that they should know a lot as British journalists, but we should be on the onslaught here, attacking their ignorance or the sinister manipulation effects and stop apologising for something we are not.' (Pappé, 2019)

Pappé (2019) moves to a full exposure of what is happening by spelling out that for the first time in the history of any mainstream political party in the West since 1948, a leader holds a pro-Palestinian position:

'This is the whole story, they thought this would never happen, it suddenly unfolded in front of their eyes, they cannot use F-16s, they cannot bomb Jeremy Corbyn, they cannot send Israeli tanks [...] to the Labour party headquarters, so they can't use the main method they usually use to silence people [...] in this case they were a bit more limited in what they could do, I must say to their, cynically I would say, to their credit, they found a way.'

In his summation, he responds to a question about the right-wing Israeli prime minister Netanyahu's rule to explain the true nature of Zionism:

'In those ten years [...] all the shields of complexity that Israel, especially the Israeli Labor Party [...] the so-called Israeli peace camp, the left Zionist camp, all these shields of complexity, where you supposedly could be a socialist and a Zionist, you could be a colonizer and an enlightened person, you could be a progressive and an ethnic cleanser, that all these impossible oxymorons, even the Israeli electorate seem to find them quite ridiculous and that's why they kicked out the Zionist Left, it doesn't exist anymore, and Netanyahu is just the epitome of this kind of inevitable [...] political development inside Israel, where you cannot really reconcile the ideology of Zionism with universal values, whether they are Marxism, socialism or even liberalism.' (Pappé, 2019)

On the question of antisemitism on the Left, Pappé (2019) thus presents an elaborate situation regarding the British Labour party in which a morally devoid, sinister and manipulative They – that is, Israel and Zionism – have exerted a global reach to launch a witch hunt to silence Jeremy Corbyn and the pro-Palestinian Left with fabricated allegations of antisemitism, creating 'a manipulated hysteria'. Beyond the use of F-16s, he states, 'they found a way' (ibid). Rather than despair at the rise of the Israeli Right, Pappé, (2019) appears to welcome its defeat of the Israeli Left, because this proves him right, apropos 'the so-called Israeli peace camp', that Zionism is the absolute antithesis of progressive universal values. In sum, he claims, antisemitism is a deceitful weapon of Zionism and Zionism is the enemy of humanity.

Miller (2020), in a public meeting titled 'In Defence of Free Speech', talks of his 'shocked, perhaps not that surprised' realisation of the complicity of the leadership of the Labour party, under Jeremy Corbyn and Jennie Formby, in the witch hunt of the Left under the false guise of antisemitism:

'They [the leadership under Jeremy Corbyn and Jennie Formby] adopted the witch hunt [...] they decided that what was going on here was people who had genuine grievances, perhaps mistaken but genuine grievances about members of the Party, and we should engage them in constructive dialogue, and of course there is no constructive dialogue with the Zionist movement.'

He then alludes to an elaborate web of global Zionist power linking Israeli ministries to a range of individuals and organisations in the UK:

'It wasn't just a question of the Zionist movement, of the trolls, of the JLM [Jewish Labour Movement], of Labour Against Antisemitism, and [...] all of that lot, you know backed of course by the Ministry of Strategic Affairs in Israel, it wasn't just a question of them [...] you see in the Labour leaked report [...] there's a bit where they discuss the people that they took on to be in charge of antisemitism investigations, one of whom is a former member of the Alliance for Workers' Liberty, a well-known [bleep] faction, and the other one says in a long passage in the report, which he himself must have written, that he learned about left antisemitism from reading a book by Dave Rich of the Community Security Trust, an organisation which has been at the forefront of pursuing the witch hunt, which is unable to distinguish between anti-Zionism and antisemitism, and which purposefully blurs together those two concepts in order to pursue the Left.' (Miller, 2020)

Miller (2021) later expands, during a conference titled 'Building the Campaign for Free Speech':

'It didn't start with the Labour party, it's not started with the Labour party and moved to the universities, it's an all-out onslaught by the Israeli government, mainly through the Ministry of Strategic Affairs, but also other ministries too, on the Left globally and this is not something which just happened in Britain [...] this is an all-out attack by the Israeli government [...] this attempt by the Israelis to impose their will all over the world and that I think is what we should recognise.'

On the ultimate Zionist enemy, he concludes:

> 'The idea that people like that should be engaged in constructive dialogue is a fantasy, these are people who must only be faced and defeated, they are supporters of Israel, of the racist policies of the Israeli government and of course of the racist foundation of the Israeli state founded of course as we know on ethnic cleansing and settler-colonialism […] the Zionist movement and the Israeli government are the enemy of the Left, the enemy of world peace and they must be directly targeted.' (Miller, 2020)

Zionism, Miller (2020, 2021) argues, is an all-powerful and infiltrating movement which is waging a war globally against the Left, and, as such, all of those complicit with Zionism 'must […] be faced and defeated' (ibid, 2020). What Miller resurrects here is the antisemitic myth that Jews are the hidden hand that manipulates the path of history and brings forth death and destruction to the world.

The complaints of antisemitism against Miller, and his subsequent dismissal by his employer, the University of Bristol, in 2021, has provoked a noticeable backlash from a mass of academics. In a letter of 'Educators and researchers in support of Professor Miller', an extensive number of academic signatories defend Miller's academic freedom at the same time as denying his antisemitism. The letter states:

> 'We oppose anti-Semitism, Islamophobia and all forms of racism. We also oppose false allegations and the weaponisation of the positive impulses of anti-racism so as to silence anti-racist debate. We do so because such vilification has little to do with defeating the harms caused by racism. Instead, efforts to target, isolate and purge individuals in this manner are aimed at deterring evidence-based research, teaching and debate. […] At a time when the Black Lives Matter movement has reinvigorated public consciousness

about the structural factors entrenching racism, attempts to stifle discourse on Islamophobia and anti-Palestinian racism are particularly regressive and inconsistent with the values the University of Bristol espouses.' (Support David Miller, 2021)

While superficially acknowledging antisemitism as a form of racism, this letter actually denies antisemitism as a form of racism by presenting antisemitism as a false cry which shamefully seeks to weaponise progressive anti-racist instincts. Genuine racism, it is made clear, is the racism challenged by Black Lives Matter and pro-Palestinian allies.

I do not find Miller's academic support base for his academic freedom problematic. Academic freedom means academics should not be dismissed for their political views. And while discriminatory or harassment behaviour could be considered grounds for dismissal, this should only follow an independent, open and transparent process, where alleviation without further harm to the victim is not possible. But what is problematic in this case is the abundance of academics who are publicly willing to deny that Miller presents antisemitic ideas and who dismiss antisemitism on the Left.

In sum, Finkelstein and Pappé do not simply meet the criteria for the Left's exceptional Jews; in some respects, they have written these criteria in their contributions to a leftist understanding of the Palestinian-Israeli conflict and the nature of Israel. Miller, who is not of Jewish background, is a more remarkable case: an outlier figure of the Left that has, as a proclaimed victim of false allegations of antisemitism, galvanised a mass academic support base that brings him closer to its centre.

I now proceed to move beyond an anti-racist imagination that casts Jews *out* as victims of racism by casting Jews *in* as the perpetrators of racism, by reintegrating anti-Jewish racism into the past-to-present development of racist ideology, including on the Left.

Chapter 2

RACISM BEYOND THE COLOUR LINE

> 'One of the regrettable features of much contemporary theorising about race and racism has been the tendency to leave the question of anti-semitism to one side, treating it almost as a separate issue.' (Back and Solomos, 2000: 191)

> 'The ghost of Israel-Palestine haunts the current separatism between racism and antisemitism.' (Cousin and Fine, 2012: 181)

Racism is an ideological way of making sense of the world (including capitalism) and its ills through the belief that there are different culturally innate 'races' with one or more 'races' harmful and a threat to one's own 'race'. The idea of 'race' in anti-Jewish racism is represented by 'the Jewish question': that something must be done about the threat that Jews pose to humanity.

The prevailing academic approach to the study of 'race' and racism effectively banishes the phenomenon of anti-Jewish racism. While Les Back and John Solomos (2000), in *Theories of Race and Racism: A Reader*, acknowledge the academic tendency to exclude antisemitism from research on racism, Glynis Cousin and Robert Fine (2012) spell out the intersecting spectre of the Palestinian-Israeli conflict, which fuels this exclusion. In this chapter, I explore the significance of a colonial model of racism to academic enquiry into 'race' and racism, both in steering attention away from anti-Jewish racism and in positioning Zionism as racism. As Robert Miles (1989: 67–68) explains:

'Much of the British and North American theorising about capitalism and racism since the 1960s, while drawing upon the immoral status of racism which derives to a significant degree from the final solution, utilises a colonial model which has little scope to explain much of the European racism of the nineteenth and twentieth centuries, and certainly not that form of racism which others label anti-semitism [...] it does, however, have a relevance to the controversial debate about whether or not Zionism can be defined as an instance of racism.'

This colonial model of racism ties racism so tightly to a history of slavery and colonialism that it translates racism into 'what powerful white people think and do to poor black and brown people'. Furthermore, when fused with analysis of the Palestinian-Israeli conflict, this model neatly interprets Zionism as a collective of 'powerful and white, racist and colonialist Jews', downplaying the historical development of Zionism as a nationalist response to murderous antisemitism and the more general overlap of nationalism with racism. This chapter presents a holistic historical perspective to contemporary racism that reintegrates consideration of anti-Jewish racism into the anti-racist imagination. For this purpose, I draw extensively on the research of the academic Marxist and sociologist Professor Robert Miles, whose publications include *Racism and migrant labour*; *White Man's Country: Racism in British Politics* (co-authored with Annie Phizacklea); *Racism after 'race relations'*; and *Racism* (co-authored with Malcolm Brown). I also use the work of the late scholar George Mosse (1918–1999) to examine the history of modern European racism leading up to Nazi Germany's final solution.

I commence this chapter with a critical examination of the colonial model of racism and its consequences for the question of antisemitism and Zionism, before turning to an alternative conceptualisation of racism as an ideology for making sense of the world. By approaching racism as an ideology, it can be understood that 'race' is an idea and an outcome of an ongoing process of racialisation: of representing 'racial' meaning to both the 'Self' and the 'threatening Other', which is shaped, over time and across space, by specific conditions of existence. I argue that the colonial model of racism problematically turns the fluid and contested idea of 'race' into a fixed 'racial' reality – implying that 'racial' culture has a natural essence and substantive political and social implications.

The problem with this colonial model is that it restricts what is considered racism to a 'white-over-black' relationship, thus removing from view anti-Jewish racism, and neglecting a wider dynamic of racism with nationalism and capitalism. This, in turn, fuels a notion of Zionism as racist colonialism that eliminates a proper analysis of Zionism as a form of nationalism – both a nationalism with racist and colonial dimensions, and a nationalism seeking to escape antisemitism.

Finally, a pre-history and a history of racism is presented, which explores the origins of racist ideology in pre-capitalist and capitalist social relations within and beyond Europe, and its reproduction vis-à-vis the rise of nation states, nationalism and colonialism. While colonialism was 'an integral moment' in the history of racism, this chapter shows that it was actually 'the articulation between the capitalist mode of production and the nation state, rather than between capitalism and colonialism' that mapped 'the primary set of social relations within which racism had its origins and initial effects' (Miles, 1993: 21). Through this history, I am able to trace anti-Jewish racism and to explain its ideological nature, including its manifestation on the contemporary Left.

THE COLONIAL MODEL OF RACISM

'By positing "race" as the subject of a theory [...], it is accorded uncritically with a reality *sui generis* which is unwarranted.' (Miles, 1993: 35)

A major contribution of Miles to the study of 'race' and racism is his critique of a dominant body of academic work that sees the origins of racism solely and exclusively in colonialism, one consequence of which is a conceptual deflation of racism to 'a "white ideology" created exclusively to dominate "blacks"' (Miles, 1993: 7; see also: Miles, 1989; Miles and Brown, 2003). This approach to racism is shown to have emerged from the rise of the civil rights movement and the increasing scale and intensity of political struggles of African-Americans against racist oppression and inequality in the United States, with Stokely Carmichael (later Kwame Ture) and Charles Hamilton's (1968) book *Black Power* pivotal in shaping academic analysis (Miles and Brown, 2003). Since the 1960s, a rising body of academics in the United States have concluded that only 'white' people are capable of racism and, subsequently, that 'white' people have limited ability to understand racism, and their involvement in anti-racism work typifies a colonising mentality that regards the victims of racism incapable of autonomous agency and resistance (Miles and Brown, 2003). For example, the US academic Robert Blauner (1969: 396) defines racism as 'a system of domination' that 'is part of the complex of colonization', and, in his book *Racial Oppression in America*, as encompassing processes that maintain 'white' domination, i.e., the 'control of whites over non-whites' (Blauner, 1972: 9–10, cited in Miles and Brown, 2003: 67). Similarly, the US academic David Wellman, in his book *Portraits of White Racism*, contends that racism is a structural relationship of 'white' racial domination over another racial group: 'white racism is what white people do to protect the special benefits they gain by virtue of their skin colour' (Wellman, 1977: 76, cited in Miles and Brown, 2003: 68).

Since the 1960s, this US approach has significantly influenced British academic thought on 'race' and racism (Miles, 1989; Miles and Brown, 2003). So, even though racism was central to the rise of fascism in western Europe during the 1930s, the concept of racism since 1945 has evolved and been largely shaped by a need to comprehend colonialism, either in a postcolonial situation or in the context of migration from the ex-colonies into western European countries (Miles and Brown, 2003). The focus of the US approach on the legacy of slavery and colonialism, including the theory of internal colonialism (which explains US capitalist society as the 'white' domination, oppression and exploitation of its 'black' and 'racial' minority populations), has transferred across the Atlantic. Consequently, British academic research has produced 'definitions and theories of racism that are so specific to the history of overseas colonisation that they have limited value in explaining any other context', with much theorising transposing the dual camp of coloniser and colonised into 'white' versus 'black' thus further limiting the explanatory power of the concept of racism (Miles and Brown, 2003). In essence, the colonial model of racism is premised on the existence of stratified 'race relations', specifically, the structural subordination of non-white populations by colonialism and internal colonialism (as the colonised have migrated from the peripheries to the centres). 'Blacks' are assumed to be the 'subordinated totality and totally subordinated' and 'whites' the 'dominant totality and totally dominant', with the implication that this 'race relation' is the primary, or indeed the sole, driver of wider social relations (Miles and Brown, 2003: 71).

Through the colonial model of racism and its deflated concept of racism, the academic anti-racist imagination continues rather than challenges racialised essentialism (that is, the idea that humankind consists of people of different 'races' with different intrinsic dispositions) and locks a divided (but otherwise universal) body of human beings into a dualistic struggle and structural bind of 'race relations'. The problem, put simply, is that 'there are no "races" and therefore no "race relations"' (Miles, 1993: 42). Instead of exploring how *the idea of 'race'* intersects with capitalist social relations, 'race' is assumed to be functional to capitalism and to form a fixed and over-totalised structure of oppression. On the face of it, work that seeks to expose the stratified 'race relations' of colonialism, imperialism and capitalism has the weight of being politically progressive. After all, by linking 'racism and capitalism functionally and causally', 'capitalism' can 'be damned for yet another reason' (Miles and Brown, 2003: 72). The problem here is the reification of the idea of 'race', that is, *'race' is made real*, rather than understanding that it is *the idea* of 'race' which has *reality*, and that needs to be explained as emerging from and shaped by fluid conditions and forces of existence.

This side of the Atlantic, Miles (1984) offers an important early challenge to the sociological research of Stuart Hall and Paul Gilroy (Centre for Contemporary Cultural Studies, 1982) and Ambalavaner Sivanandan – which retains the idea of 'race' as a descriptive and analytical concept thus giving 'race' an analytical reality and primacy in determining people's experience and material position. Miles (1984: 230) makes clear, 'the "black masses" are not a "race"', but rather are people whose political struggles need to be understood in terms of processes of racialisation within their specific class relations. 'Perversely', Miles and Brown (2003: 90) state, North American and European 'social scientists have prolonged the life of an idea that should be consigned to the dustbin of analytically useless terms'. It is worth noting that Gilroy, while distancing himself from Miles, later arrives at a similar position to him. In Gilroy's (1998: 839) seminal paper, 'Race ends here', he argues for 'a more consistent effort to de-nature and de-ontologize "race"'. This change of course is all the more important, he recognises, because 'the memory of the Nazi genocide has ceased to form the constellation under which we strive to do critical work in this area' (ibid: 839). In other words, by making 'race' real, the lens of what is racism in critical research on 'race' no longer sees antisemitism.

The colonial model of racism is primarily a cultural analysis of racism (that interprets racism as cultural phenomena, representations and practices), which has contributed to the development of postcolonial and colonial discourse theories, such as Edward Said's (1995) *Orientalism* thesis, and a conscious distancing from Marxist analysis of capitalist political economy and class relations (Miles and Brown, 2003). From this, a crude moralisation and generalisation of racism has emerged, rather than a more nuanced approach to racism which considers how the idea of 'race' interrelates with capitalism in fluid and contested ways. With the history of slavery, for example, it is easy to presume the fusion of racism to slavery's functioning. However, as a mode of production, slavery did not necessarily depend on racism and existed prior to it (Miles and Brown, 2003). Barker's (1978) study, *The African Link: British Attitudes to the Negro in the Era of the Atlantic Slave Trade, 1550–1807*, shows that the Atlantic slave trade represented a significant stage in the development of racist ideas, specifically, in the racist animus developed during New World slavery and the racist knowledge produced and widely distributed on 'black' Africa. Nonetheless, the late eighteenth century abolition debate, Barker (1978: 198) reveals, had 'far more' defenders of slavery 'who pointedly rejected racialism' than the 'handful of pro-slavery racialists'.

The immorality of racism rooted in the notion of 'white' colonial power, Miles (1989) warns, has serious implications for an understanding of both antisemitism and Zionism. Indeed, while the colonial model of racism 'condemn[s] "white" people to a universal condition that implies possession of a permanent essence that inevitably sets them apart' (Miles and Brown, 2003: 75), in the case of 'white' Jews associated with Zionism and Israel, this racist essentialism is taken a step further in the claim that Zionism is an exceptional racism that weaponises antisemitism. For example, the postcolonial theorist Patrick Wolfe (2016: 18), in his book *Traces of History: Elementary Structures of Race*, defines racism as a European colonial invention and project, in which the different 'regimes of race' have in common 'Whiteness' and the prime objective of 'White supremacy'. Wolfe (2016: 110) does two things to antisemitism and Zionism in his analysis of 'race': antisemitism is relegated to history, and (he purports) this trace of racism is kept alive in Zionism, specifically, through Zionism's channelling of past antisemitism into the racist exclusion of Palestinians:

'[Zionism] retained the racial topography that it shared with antisemitism and sought to protect it, structurally intact, to another country. [...] the regime of race that Zionism sought to impose in Palestine retained and redirected the Judeophobic trace – the project of exclusion – that Zionism shared with antisemitism in Europe.'

In Wolfe's (2016: 203) structural framework of colonial and postcolonial 'race relations', Zionism is 'unparalleled' in its racist planning and execution. This echoes the arguments made by Said (1995) in *Orientalism*, in which he asserts that Orientalism – as 'the formidable structure of cultural domination' (25) – makes 'every European, in what he [*sic*] could say about the Orient, [...] a racist, an imperialist, and almost totally ethnocentric' (204). Contemporary anti-Arab racism is described by Said (1995: 286) as 'the transference' of past antisemitic 'animus' from the Jews to the Arabs – the Arab 'conceived of now as a shadow that dogs the Jew'. In sum, deriving in part from the colonial model of racism, there is a tendency on the academic Left to dismiss the idea that Jews still suffer from racism, and to instead see 'white and powerful Jews', embodied in and who embody Israel and Zionism, using and abusing their past victimhood of racist persecution as part of an unprecedented racism against 'black/brown and powerless' Palestinians. Moreover, the postcolonial approach to the Palestinian-Israeli conflict, which I explore and critique in Chapter Three, illustrates the co-existence of the colonial model of racism with 'the Jewish question' (the idea of the Jewish collective as harmful to humanity), such that, Jews are represented as both racist colonisers, and *the* historical outliers of a decolonisation era and *the* global pioneers and exporters of racist oppression.

CONCEPTUALISING RACISM

By seeing racism as a fixed doctrine, which the colonial model of racism does, rather than as a fluid and contested ideology intersecting with capitalist social relations, racism is conceptualised as a rigid structure of oppression fused to capitalism. As a doctrine, the relationship between racism and capitalism is deterministic: racism serves capitalism, capitalism fuels 'white privilege', and anti-racism is a necessary anti-capitalist damnation of racists.

By contrast, as an ideology, the relationship of racism and capitalism is something to be comprehended through investigation, and anti-racism is the challenge of racist *ideas* – after all, 'individuals are not racist', 'it is an ideology that is racist' (Miles and Brown, 2003: 109). Drawing on Antonio Gramsci's concept of common-sense ideology, Miles and Brown (2003: 105) explain:

> 'An emphasis on racism solely as a "false doctrine" fails to appreciate that one of the conditions of existence of ideologies (which by definition constitute in their totality a false explanation, but which may nevertheless also incorporate elements of truth) is that they can successfully "make sense" of the world, at least for those who articulate and use them.'

Racism has traction because it offers a seeming solution to real world problems. Anti-immigration racism among currents of the working class might appear to address the problem of a shortage of well-paid jobs or affordable housing, for example. Gramsci (1971) recognises that people make sense of the world and the 'specific problems posed by reality' (324) through a '"spontaneous philosophy"' (323) or 'contradictory consciousness' (333). People's ideas tend to be, in the first instance, 'not critical and coherent but disjointed and episodic', deriving from groups with opposing outlooks (ibid: 324). Embryonic 'good sense' is the healthy nucleus of an anti-dialectical and dogmatic 'common sense' (Gramsci, 1971: 323), consisting of 'prejudices from all past phases of history' that have 'left stratified deposits in popular philosophy' (ibid: 324). 'Vulgar common sense' induces a state of submissiveness and conformity, exploiting eagerness 'for peremptory certainties' (Gramsci, 1971: 435). Racism demonstrates how commonsense appears to be 'a specific way of rationalising the world and real life' (ibid: 337) albeit 'a creation of concrete phantasy' (ibid: 126). The notion of contradictory consciousness (in which two contradictory sets of ideas co-exist) explains how people can have racist ideas by not fully questioning these ideas or realising their own agency as a collective working class to provide alternative answers to social problems. Hegemonic racist conditions do not exist through a neat structure of social control or process of social consent, but rather by grudging and partial acquiescence. Racism is not a fixed state. Gramsci (1971: 350) recognises the role of organic intellectuals – socialists and anti-racists – in stimulating an 'active and reciprocal' dialogue with people to challenge common-sense and develop embryonic good-sense into the formation of a critical philosophy of the universal working class. In other words, racism as a common-sense ideology can, and must, be overcome in the battle of ideas.

Crucially, for all racism, it is a process of racialisation, as 'a dialectical process of signification', that characterises and organises human beings into distinct and opposing 'racial' groups of Self and Other, and creates the idea of 'race' (Miles and Brown, 2003: 101):

> 'The moment of racism as ideology is one in which Self and Other simultaneously embrace and repel by reference to a set of imagined attributes that carry a duality of evaluations, negative and

positive. Conceptually, this is its unity. But, historically, the ideological content, the specific groups represented as Self and Other, and the consequences are always diverse.' (Ibid: 86)

Racism is an ideological distortion of how one sees human beings and social relations which has and is capable of drawing upon a range of indicators of self-perpetuating 'racial' difference and inferiority/superiority.

Once it is understood that racism is the outcome of a process of racialisation that identifies Other 'racial' groups as a collective threat and harm to the Self, then an open enquiry can commence into the production and reproduction of meaning. Indeed, such enquiry would reveal that racism is not confined to colonial origins. Take, for example, the racialised notion of civilisation, which was a central discursive justification for European colonisation of the non-European world. This notion was reproduced in colonialism but did not originate from it. The civilising mission, Miles (1993) shows, originated within feudal Europe and from the processes of social differentiation initiated by the ruling class to legitimise their rule, which, subsequently, with the spread of capitalist relations of production, developed to connect the interior with the exterior of the European world. The French aristocracy, for example, mobilised the idea of '*politesse* and *civilité*' to contrast their refined behaviour with those they ruled over, who were considered 'the "inferior" people' (Miles, 1993: 90). During the nineteenth century, the peasantry of southern and western France were observed by scholars and politicians as savages and barbarians, whose material conditions of existence were a result of their inner nature and their 'race' apart (ibid). The Parisian bourgeoisie of the early nineteenth century, influenced by phrenology and its key role in scientific racism, commonly understood the working class through assumed 'differences of "race"', specifically, as 'a distinct physical type' with 'a set of somatic characteristics which expressed their supposed physical and moral degeneration' (Miles, 1993: 93).

On occasion, these representations went as far as the association of the working class with animal features to symbolise their purported sub-humanity (ibid). The point here is that racism – and its civilising mission – has not only been integral to colonialism, it has also been fundamental to the legitimisation of ruling-class rule and nation-state building, and the creation and advancement of capitalist social relations, inside and beyond Europe.

The colonial model of racism's reification of 'race' and 'race relations' (which makes the abstract idea of 'race' into a supposedly concrete and real difference among humankind) is also a reification of skin colour – the 'white' coloniser versus the 'black' colonised – which restricts the consideration of racism to 'white-over-black' relations in colonial, postcolonial and internal colonial settings, to the exclusion of both colonised populations beyond this colour line and non-colonised populations. Demonstrating the consequences of this conceptual deflation of racism is the case of the US Johnson-Lodge Immigration Act of 1924, which was the result of a campaign in the early twentieth century to exclude Italian, Polish, Russian, and Jewish populations from Europe in order to prevent 'racial' mixing and deterioration. These populations were considered, with evidence from psychologists, inferior 'races' with naturally inferior intelligence, in contrast to the preferentially treated British, German and Scandinavian 'stock' (Miles and Brown, 2003). Through a colonial model of racism, Robert Blauner's emphasis on racism as 'white' domination leads him to desist analysing the ideologies justifying the exclusion of Italians and Jews from the United States during the 1920s as racism: 'these populations are described as "white ethnics" who were "viewed racially" ([Blauner] 1992: 64)' (Miles and Torres, 1999: 28). Furthermore:

> 'Concerning the period of fascism in Germany, Blauner refers to genocide "where racial imagery was obviously intensified" (1992: 64), but presumably the imagery could never be intensified to the

point of warranting description as racism because the Jews were not "black".' (Miles and Torres, 1999: 28)

In addition to ruling out as racism oppressive and exclusionary phenomena which do not fit the 'white-over-black' dichotomy, the reification of skin colour in the colonial model of racism's anti-racist imagination makes the abstraction of 'race', which is an idea that has real-world consequences, into a reality as a naturalised concrete force. Following colonial and postcolonial discourse theories, and a cultural analysis of racism, in Wolfe's (2016) claim that settler-colonialism has in common Whiteness and the primary objective of White supremacy, the reification here is that there are 'white' people whose natural disposition is to dominate 'black' people. In other words, settler-colonialism is understood to be structurally driven by 'race' and 'race relations' and is assumed *to be* determined by 'race' and 'race relations'. Contrary to this approach, our job as academics is to de-fetishise 'race'. The relationship between slavery, colonialism and racism, as such, is not something to be presumed in a homogenous and fixed form, but to be known and understood through investigation of empirical reality. In this vein, Miles and Brown (2003) evidence how, from the midseventeenth to early twentieth centuries, European colonialism shared in common the occupation and settlement of land beyond their respective nation states, and the organisation of commodity production and exchange on a global scale. Concurrently, European representations of the Other were made and remade at the interface of relations of production with populations deemed culturally different. Modes of production emerged from colonialism that, unlike the commodity production and commodification of labour-power in Europe, were typified by unfree labour (Miles and Brown, 2003). In the specific case of colonial Kenya, dialectically related processes of dispossession of the means of production and racialisation created a labouring class. In other words, it is shown that racism *became* a relation of production because it was 'historically conducive to the constitution and reproduction of a system of commodity production', and thus it shaped the relationship between the exploiter and the exploited (Miles and Brown, 2003: 129).

It is important to grasp the slippage between culture and biology in racist ideology that is achieved through cultural essentialism, because it is from this recognition that one is more able to see the fundamental danger with the reification of 'race' and skin colour in the colonial model of racism and anti-racist imagination. Racism works by naturalising socially constructed differences, including cultural differences. Ethnic cleansing is both an extreme and clear demonstration of this point, as Miles and Brown (2003: 93–94) elucidate:

> '"Ethnic cleansing" was added to the lexicon in the early 1990s to denote mass murder and forced migration within the conflicts in Bosnia and Herzegovina, and other parts of the Balkans. There, the ethnic groups were identified as Serbian, Croatian, Bosnian Muslim, Romani ("Gypsy") and Albanian. In this context, phenotypical indicators of ethnicity were less important than cultural, linguistic or religious ones, but the use of mass rape as an instrument of war suggests that "other" ethnic groups were perceived as biologically distinct and self-perpetuating, and that this distinctiveness and self-perpetuation could be negated by forced insemination.'

In this case, the distinction between the concepts of ethnic difference and 'racial' difference 'is entirely elusive' (ibid: 94). The crucial point here is that the racist imagination does not require skin colour as a marker of signification to the existence of harmful 'races', because *'people do not see "race"'*: 'rather, they observe certain combinations of real and sometimes imagined somatic and cultural characteristics, to which they attribute meaning with the idea of "race"' (Miles and Torres, 1999: 32).

Indeed, as the French academic Colette Guillemin (1999) reveals, along with the apparent physical characteristics of different 'racial' groups, during the first half of the nineteenth century, other 'racial' denominators that were social and cultural traits began to emerge. From philological research, for instance, the identification of different language groups very quickly became part of the 'racial' systems of somatic classification; 'it was a short step from' here to the idea of Indo-European and Semitic 'races' (Guillemin, 1999: 41). In brief, the concept of 'race' was historically produced and reproduced from a wide range of sources and types of classification, which merged 'heterogenous lines of thought' into the singular belief that human beings are divisible by nature (ibid: 41). Through a colonial model of racism and the reification of 'race' and skin colour, academics focusing on the negative racialisation of somatic difference exclusively see only some forms of racism. However, when the racist imagination classifies 'race', the indicators chosen are 'a matter of politics rather than objective reality', as illustrated by 'the Nazis deciding who was (and was not) a Jew [...] or the government of the Republic of South Africa classifying Chinese people as belonging to one race and Japanese to another' (Guillamin, 1999: 40). 'Racial' classification is based on social imagination and political decision-making, not real innate differences between human beings. Variation of skin colour does not imply a differential essence among humankind, but the idea of 'race' activates the idea of a differential essence. Furthermore, if the colonial model of racism and its 'white-over-black' dualism renders other forms of racism invisible, this model seems particularly ill-equipped to see racism that works on the very idea of the invisible 'enemy within'. While the Jewish Other has been racialised physically by 'the hooked nose, shifty eyes, protruding ears, elongated body, flat feet, and moist hands' (Mosse, 1985: 156), the Jewish Other has also been racialised as an invisible threat. The absence of visibility here has been used to the advantage of the racist imagination:

> 'The very fact that there are so few living Jews can become socially accepted as proof of either the real extent of "Jewish power" or of the continued success of Jews in assimilating themselves, of "hiding" in order to continue their "destructive" work.' (Miles, 1993: 14)

Over the final three sections of this chapter, an alternative historical context to the colonial model of racism will be presented which enables the contemporary anti-racist imagination to comprehend and challenge racism in all of its ideological manifestations, including anti-Jewish racism. As a concept over time and space, it is illustrated that racism is both continuous and fluid, such that 'any one instance of racism' is 'the product of both a reworking of at least some of the substance of earlier instances, and a creation of novel elements' (Miles and Brown, 2003: 109).

A PRE-HISTORY OF RACISM AND THE PRECURSOR TO ANTI-JEWISH RACISM

The discourse and ideology of 'race' and its incorporation into science did not break from and replace earlier representations of the Other, including, notably, the Muslim Other and the Jewish Other, rather, European 'racial' science emerged from a context where existing patterns of 'representation and inferiorisation' were 'incorporated and theorised by new criteria of secularised validity' (Miles and Brown, 2003: 52). Put simply, the origins of racism lie much earlier than in the history of colonialism, and the historical development of racism cannot be comprehended from its 'racial' scientific career alone. Over thousands of years, production and trade, military activity and travel have fuelled a dialectical generation and reproduction of representations of the Other vis-à-vis the Self: a categorisation of human beings into different groups based on imagined differences. Miles and Brown (2003) trace a pre-history to the idea of 'race' – a major precursor to the

Enlightenment's 'racial' scientific moment – from the Greco-Roman period onwards, and from inside and outside Europe. Throughout this time, the combination of representational elements has been subject to change with certain elements remaining constant. This section overviews this pre-history to demonstrate how racism, and specifically anti-Jewish racism, developed – a view that is excluded from a perspective that traces racism from exclusively colonial origins.

Greco-Roman thought held to the notion of unity of the human species: diverse but with commonality that sets humans apart from animals and gods. Class and sex divisions nonetheless persisted, along with the idea of barbarians beyond the borders of the Greco-Roman world (Miles and Brown, 2003). The African population, for example, was signified as different through physical markers such as nose shape, hair type and skin colour. Black was associated with death and the underworld. However, not all representations of Africans were based on negative stereotypes; some saw Africans bearing capacity for wisdom and freedom. Phenotypical and cultural differences were explained as determined by physical environmental conditions (Miles and Brown, 2003).

Representations of the Other from the Greco-Roman world were reproduced in medieval Europe – combining environmental determinism (the theory that the physical environment determines a population's traits) with popular religious connotations. For example, the classification of natural events into *portenta* or *monstra*, and as reflecting God's will, was carried over from the Greco-Roman world into the Middle Ages, where entire populations, who were seen as marked by unusual phenotypical characteristics, were understood as *monstra* and through a sense of divine will (Miles and Brown, 2003). Moreover, the idea of *monstra* featured centrally in European expansion, with the Christian symbolic dichotomy of Self/Other as good/evil, spiritual/carnal, and Christ/Satan blending with the colour symbolic dichotomy of white/black (Miles and Brown, 2003).

Prior to the colonisation of the Americas (which followed the synthesis of feudal monarchies and merchant capital in Western Europe), for several centuries, the major external focus of European powers was the Arab or Muslim world (Miles and Brown, 2003). Given the major role of Christianity in legitimising feudal class power in Europe, Islam was positioned as a theological and political threat. By the fourteenth century, the rise and dominance of the Ottoman Turks was signified into the idea of the degenerate, tyrannical and barbaric Muslim Other. Culminating in the Crusades, Islam was represented as an aggressive and sexually permissive force propagating holy war against non-Muslims, while promising its devotees an afterlife in the garden of sexual pleasures. It was only by the late seventeenth century that the Muslim world was no longer considered an external threat to Europe; nevertheless, the idea of unrestrained Muslim sexuality remained (Miles and Brown, 2003). Religion was central to early representations of the Other because it was the hegemonic frame of reference for explaining and structuring the material world, but these representations were not exclusively couched in religious terms. While Islam was regarded as the anthesis of Christianity, the representational opposition between Christian Europe and the Muslim world was a 'primarily religious discourse in quasi-"racial" terms' (Miles and Brown, 2003: 29). Furthermore, the Crusades often did not differentiate the Other between Muslims, Jews and pagans.

Along with the Muslim Other, the Jewish Other was significant. From the Greco-Roman period and Roman occupation of Palestine, the early representation of Jews as a hostile Other and threat to the Roman Empire was on the basis that their monotheistic religion rejected Roman gods and the divine rule of the Emperor (Miles and Brown, 2003). This negative representation remained constant into the Christianisation of the Empire under Constantine, but the reason changed: Jews were now to blame for the death of Jesus Christ. In the period of medieval and Reformation Europe, especially during the Crusades, Jewish people were the target of economic exclusion and violence (Miles and Brown, 2003). The shift from anti-Judaism to antisemitism was neither a simple progression nor a clean break: anti-Jewish racism came into existence as a result of the growth of secularisation and nationalism, and because "'a theologically condemned caste already existed'", which could be made into the imaginary of a Jewish 'race' (Poliakov, 1975: 458–459, cited into Miles and Brown, 2003: 30–31). Furthermore, while Christian anti-Judaism kept open the possibility of conversion, modern antisemitism 'salvaged' itself 'from the assault of modern equality', as Zygmunt Bauman (1989: 59) puts it (echoing Hannah Arendt), by replacing Judaism with Jewishness.

By the end of the fifteenth century, the consolidated economic and political power of the emergent nation states of northern and western Europe shaped a new context for representations of the Other. Trade and exploration led to European contact with populations outside Europe:

'Up to this point, the non-Muslim Other (the crucial exception being the Jews […]) was outside the European arena. Moreover, discourse about the Muslim Other was for a long time generated in the context of European subordination to a greater economic and military force.' (Miles and Brown, 2003: 32)

Direct relationships between a class of Europeans with indigenous populations outside Europe came as a result of the expansion of European nation states to incorporate other areas of the world into a system of international trade and colonisation. This was structured by land competition, the initiation of private property rights, demand for labour-power, and the supposed need for conversion to Christianity – together 'embodied in the discourse of "civilisation"' (Miles and Brown, 2003: 33). Although representations of the Other varied in the accounts of missionary work, military activity, travel and trade – with positive representations based on prelapsarian fantasies – in general, the populations that Europeans came into contact with were signified negatively and formed part of a hierarchical categorisation that used the Other as evidence of European superiority (Miles and Brown, 2003). In brief, 'these representations refracted a purpose' (Miles and Brown, 2003: 36). While representations of the Other were neither homogenous nor fixed (because European colonisations had their own individual characters and courses), a notable commonality was the representation of the colonised as having excessive and untamed sexuality. African populations were generally represented by the British in animalistic and physical terms, as savage and barbaric, with environmental determinism providing the dominant explanation during much of the seventeenth and eighteenth centuries (Miles and Brown, 2003). These early representations of the Other provided, as the next section will discuss, the ideological conditions for the revision of the Other in 'racial' terms. As Miles and Brown (2003: 40) observe, the development of 'racial' science did not substitute earlier conceptions of the Other for its modern production of the racialised Other, rather, the ideas of 'savagery, barbarism and civilisation', which are found in early representations of the Other, both 'predetermined the space that the idea of "race" occupied' and 'were themselves reconstituted by it.'

A HISTORY OF MODERN RACISM

Although 'racial' science was a challenge to Christian representations of the Other, many 'racial' scientists of the eighteenth and nineteenth centuries were able to maintain that 'racial' difference was consistent with Christian theology. Moreover, 'racial' science did not present coherently: 'each attempt at classification broke down under the weight of logical inconsistency and empirical evidence', prior to a new classification being made (Miles and Brown, 2003: 41). A crucial insight provided by the scholarship of Mosse (1985) is that modern racism was an outcome of both the Enlightenment, in the search for a scientific truth to 'race', and the religious revivalism of the eighteenth century, in the mystical quest for the pure 'racial' soul:

> '[Racism] was a product of the preoccupation with a rational universe, nature, and aesthetics, as well as with the emphasis upon the eternal force of religious emotion and man's [*sic*] soul. It was part, too, of the drive to define man's place in nature and of the hope for an ordered, healthy, and happy world. Eventually, the racist outlook fused man's outward appearance with his place in nature and the proper functioning of his soul. Thus, religious emotion became integrated in racism as part of the "racial soul."' (Mosse, 1985: 3)

In this respect, the religious notion of a 'chain of being' became a secularised focus of 'racial' scientific work. Even when the belief in angels had passed, integrated into scientific enquiry of 'race' was an understanding of human beings as part of nature and a need to find the 'missing link' that connected human beings to animals; indeed, 'the highest animal, usually thought to be the ape, reached out during the eighteenth century to the lowest kind of man, usually thought to be black' (Mosse, 1985: 4). This blend of science and mysticism explains why aesthetics (i.e., the ideal of beauty) became a central principle of 'racial' classification, because it 'bridged the gap' between the Enlightenment's drive for rationalism and knowledge and the spiritual search for signs that could overcome the feelings of alienation and confusion that came from a period of rapid change (Mosse, 1985: 11). In contrast to the centrality of change in the scientific outlook, aesthetics provided the ideology of racism with a desired sense of timelessness and need to make sense of origins amid tumultuous change (Mosse, 1985). Increasing contact with the Other, specifically, African populations outside Europe and Jews as a newly emancipated minority within Europe, strengthened the foundations of modern racism. That said, while a consistent, negative 'racial' representation of black populations was made (seen to be fixed low in the chain of being), it was only after the mid-nineteenth century that racism was consistently applied to Jewish populations (Mosse, 1985).

From the mid-nineteenth century, Mosse (1985: 34) notes, 'the ideal human stereotype' was 'complete', leading to the coalescence of racism and nationalism – popularly expressed in the interchangeable use of the terms 'people', 'race' and 'nation'. Indeed, as Miles (1993: 62) states: 'The "nation" was imagined less as a "people" bound together by a common interest in the overthrow of political domination by an absolute monarch or an autocratic landed aristocracy (or both), and more as a population defined primarily by a certain language, set of customs and discrete historical origin (Hobsbawn 1990: 19–22). In such circumstances, the "nation" was increasingly constructed in opposition to "foreigners", both inside and beyond the territory.'

The groundwork for the co-creation of racism and nationalism was laid from the eighteenth century, specifically, with the development of anthropology and the pseudosciences of physiognomy and phrenology, and, by the turn of the eighteenth to nineteenth centuries, with a new interest in history and linguistics (Mosse, 1985). The search for linguistic origins was motivated by an effort to reveal the origins of 'race', with philologists concluding that Sanskrit was the basis for all Western languages, brought over to Europe from Asia by the Aryan people; here the term Aryan first appears (Mosse, 1985). For a period of time, India's Aryan origins were exceptionalised as 'racial' excellence, in contrast to Jews and Arabs who were seen as incapable of creating epic poetry. But, by the mid-nineteenth century, enquiry into 'racial' origins started to focus on Scandinavia rather than Asia, and Indians were subsequently excluded from the Aryan 'race'. 'Racial' science classified the existence within Europe of various 'races', notably, Nordic, Roman, Gallic, and Anglo-Saxon, with language frequently being the central signifier of an imagined national community and the manifestation of 'race' (Miles and Brown, 2003). Language was seen to represent the ideals of honour, nobility and courage (Mosse, 1985), and framed the growing nationalist and racist intolerance towards populations considered not to share common Aryan origins and incapable of managing the native tongue:

> 'It became usual in anti-Semitic works for Jews to speak a mixture of German and Yiddish, a "jargon" from which not even a Rothschild could escape. The linguistic abilities of African Negroes were treated with similar contempt.' (Mosse, 1985: 44)

Indeed, the famous 'racial' theorist Comte Arthur de Gobineau made extensive use of linguistic theories and the myth of the Aryan 'race'. Further overlap in national and 'racial' signification derived from the idea that different groups of peoples carried different capacities and desires for freedom. The modern nationalisms of Europe competed over who had the strongest innate drive for freedom:

> 'Those who did not share these roots were inferior precisely because they did not know freedom and therefore wanted to enslave the world. This was a major accusation against the Jews. The urge toward acquiring power over others was thought inherent in their lack of spirituality. […] The Negroes, in turn, could not know true freedom because they were thought incapable of forming a true community in the first place.' (Mosse, 1985: 49–50)

As stressed in the work of Gobineau, while Jews 'longed only for domination', black people were incapable of even this, since they 'lived in chaos' (Mosse, 1985: 50). In essence, 'race' and nation were conceptualised during a time of internal reorganisation of European political economies and external European expansion, which brought Europeans directly and indirectly into contact with a wider range of assumed differences between human beings, as such, the two ideologies had the potential to fuse:

> 'This potential was grounded in the very nature of scientific racism which asserted a deterministic link between biology and cultural variation/expression. Because "nations" were identified as naturally occurring groups identifiable by cultural *differentiae*, it was logically possible to assert that these symbols of "nation" were themselves grounded in "race".' (Miles, 1987: 30)

The ideas of 'race' and nation, Miles and Brown (2003: 147) state, 'were not so much identical (Mosse 1978: 45) as mutual reflections'.

The trajectory of racist ideology shown by Gobineau (and continued by others) was metapolitical: that is, based on the view that the political process arises 'from the subconscious of the Volk or race' (Mosse, 1985: 65). Drawing on anthropology, linguistics and history, Gobineau argued, in his *Essay on the Inequality of Human Races, 1853–55*, that the world was composed of different civilisations, which were determined by 'race', not environment. He identified three 'races', white, yellow and black, and pitched a drama of degeneration on the basis that it was no longer possible for any 'race' to stay pure: 'the white race was becoming more like the yellow peoples in its materialism and more like the blacks as a mob' (Mosse, 1985: 54). Unlike Gobineau, his successor Comte Georges Vacher de Lapouge attempted to base 'racial' ideology in science. In his work, de Lapouge claimed that: 'the inferior races such as the yellow race and the Jews were without scruples and had no sense of values, being wholly commercial. [...] Aryan commercial society lives by honest work. The Aryans care about the values with which they speculate; but the Jew loves speculation for its own sake' (Mosse, 1985: 60).

Crucially here is an idea that ricochets down the tunnel of anti-Jewish racist ideology: that Jews are immoral capitalists who make money in devious ways, rather than, like the Aryans, by honest work. The idea of the deceitful Jew, who exists in contrast to honest capitalism, arises also in the contribution to racism from English intellectuals, which came through Darwinism and the eugenics movement, as well as from linguistics, history and anthropology. Social Darwinism linked the idea of 'race' to evolutionary theory and survival of the fittest, with 'racial' eugenics intellectually developed by Francis Galton's theory of heredity (Mosse, 1985). Enquiry in the latter half of the nineteenth century was preoccupied with the origins of the Anglo-Saxon 'race' and proving that the qualities of love of freedom, honesty and loyalty were innate solely to the Anglo-Saxon 'race' (Mosse, 1985). While Gobineau's 'racial' enemy fixated on black populations, for the Scottish 'racial' scientist Robert Knox (author of *Races of Man*), the enemy was the Jew, and his racialisation drew on aesthetics:

'Knox's Jews were ugly [...] and even a superficially beautiful Jewish face could not withstand close scrutiny for want of proportion. The perfect type of man [*sic*] discovered by the sculptors of ancient Greece had found its foil. This stereotype was not unique, but Knox went further than most [...] the Jew had no occupation at all, but like the gypsy, lived by cunning alone.' (Mosse, 1985: 68–69)

Knox, like de Lapouge, develops on the theme that contrasts the honest and hard-working Aryan bourgeoisie to that of the Jew, who reflects 'the distorted image of the bourgeoisie – cunning, scheming, and usurious' (Mosse, 1985: 69). Amid the challenge to Britain's global dominance from competing European capitalisms, 'each embodied in a separate national shell, and each seeking its "destiny" on the world stage' (Miles, 1993: 68), by the end of the nineteenth century, a new English patriotic racism emerged. This racism signified the whole world, including Europe. One consequence of this English racism was the agitation for immigration controls that further racialised the Jews. Subsequently, beginning just prior to the close of the nineteenth century, political agitation against immigration from eastern Europe began, with the everyday association of immigrant and alien with 'the Jew'. Jewishness was increasingly understood in terms of 'race' and thus as immutable and heredity. Furthermore, the Jewish 'race' was signified as 'an alien presence that had the potential to destroy civilised society through the promotion of an international conspiracy' – in sum, 'the Jews became the racialised "enemy within"' (Miles, 1993: 135–136). The accusations during this time of the Jews as criminals, living a perverted sexual lifestyle, and existing exclusively, became sustained and prominent 'racial' characteristics.

Two traditions of the nineteenth century were brought over in the racism that evolved into the twentieth century: 'The mystical idea of race, which extended the ever present subjectivity of racial thought until it left any pretence of science behind; and that tradition which sought scientific and academic respectability for racial classification' (Mosse, 1985: 77).

'Racial' scientists endeavoured for empirical proofs so tended towards ambivalence at the use of racism for political projects of 'racial' superiority or aggression. Nevertheless, a new urgency shaped the production of 'racial' scientific knowledge, deriving from the associated anxieties at the accelerated speed of urbanisation and population growth in western and central Europe. A popular belief developed that if the 'ideas of natural selection and heredity were not translated into practice', 'a catastrophe might result' (Mosse, 1985: 78). The language of both 'racial' scientists and the German National Socialist party, for example, spoke of the fear of degeneration. It is in this context that Mosse (2000: 195–196) understands the connection between past antisemitism and emergent modern anti-Jewish racism:

'The mystery of race transformed the Jew into an evil principle. This was nothing new for the Jew; after all, anti-Christ had been a familiar figure during the Middle Ages. But in the last decades of the nineteenth century and the first half of the twentieth, the traditional legends which had swirled about the Jews in the past were revived as foils for racial mysticism and as instruments of political mobilization. Accusations of ritual murder, the curse of Ahasverus the wandering Jew, and fantasies about the universal Jewish world conspiracy had never vanished from the European consciousness even during the Enlightenment. Now they were to be revitalized and given renewed force. [...] These legends, whether the blood libel or that of the wandering Jew, offered explanation and coherence in a world of industrialization, instability, and bewildering social change, just as they had earlier been used as explanation for famines, sickness, and all manner of natural catastrophes.'

Critically, the 'line between Christian anti-Semitism and racism', Mosse (2000: 199) explains, 'was thin', after all:

'There was no need for secular nationalism to confront the problem of how Jews could be changed into Christians through baptism if their race was inherently evil, nor was it necessary as a part of the drama of Christian salvation to disentangle the Jews of the Old Testament from their inferior racial status. All racists did better to ignore Christianity whenever possible. In this regard, a journalist like Wilheim Marr in Germany was typical. His *Jewry's Victory over Teutonism* ([...] 1879) rejected the Christian accusations against the Jews as unworthy of the enlightened, but then repeated all the myths about rootless and conspiratorial Jews.'

Medieval and Christian allegations against the Jews were not discarded, rather 'they became intertwined with the fear of finance capitalism and the deprivations of modern society' (Mosse, 1985: 148). Along with the association of Jews with animal imagery, placing them low in the chain of being, the *Protocols of the Elders of Zion* reinforced the racialisation of Jews with immoral materialism:

> 'In the eerie setting of the cemetery, the elders conspire to take over the world. They plot to concentrate all capital into their hands; to secure possession of all land, railroads, mines, houses; to occupy government posts; to seize the press and direct all public opinion.' (Mosse, 2000: 197)

Above all else, anti-Jewish racism ideologically served 'those who wanted to reinvigorate the national mystique by emphasizing equality among the people' by using 'the Jews as a foil' (Mosse, 2000: 200). The French journalist Edouard Drumont advanced the idea of 'the mercantile, covetous, scheming, and cunning Semites' who 'were responsible for the existing state of national and social degeneration' (Mosse, 1985: 155). German National Socialism directed animosity towards the dominance of finance capitalism (banking and the stock exchange) and the Jews who symbolised this, claiming that the 'abolition of the "slavery of interest charges" would produce both social justice and national unity' (Mosse, 1985: 151). This recurrent distinction in anti-Jewish racism between money made from honest sweat and toil and money made by unscrupulous means, and the association of Jews with exploitative unproductive labour and deviant capitalism, was not exclusive to the political Right. For the French utopian socialist Alphonso Toussenel and French anarchist Pierre-Joseph Proudhon, the 'race' of the Jews 'was predatory, competitive, and without morality, and was therefore to be excluded from participating in a genuinely national and socialist community' (Mosse, 1985: 154).

The First World War was decisive in determining the fate of racism, of which anti-Jewish racism was central: it had the effect of transforming racism from a theory into a practice. The soldiers of the First World War symbolised the ideal Self, carrying the virtues of camaraderie, activism and heroism, while the Jewish Other (the revolutionaries, Freemasons and capitalist exploiters) were the enemy and hostile threat; with 'one kind of death reserved for the man [*sic*] who fought for the nation, and another for the enemy' (Mosse, 1985: 175). The increasing wave of nationalism fused with anti-Jewish racism and pitched the Jewish Other – 'a people without roots' (Mosse, 2000: 200) – as the ultimate threat to the nation. The need for national unity along with the influence of spiritualism from the United States into Europe meant that: 'The mythological and spiritual roots of the race were equated with the national origins: the past of race and its history was identical with the history of the nation' (Mosse, 1985: 94).

Under German National Socialism: 'The myth of Ahasverus, the wandering Jew who wants to destroy Germany through Bolshevism, and who is waiting to rejoice at the desolation of Europe, was evoked and presented as reality. The war Hitler unleashed would be blamed upon the Jews, who would then be destroyed' (Mosse, 1985: 214).

Hitler's racism was based on the belief that he was leading a cosmic warfare between the Aryan and the Jew with the objective of achieving a living space for Germany through the final solution (Mosse 1985). In other words, the Jewish people posed a threat to the nation state on the basis of their existence as a diaspora: the presence of the Jews jeopardised the very idea of a natural link between people and homeland (*Volk* and *Land*) and threatened the expansionist destiny of the nation state (Miles and Brown, 2003). As Bauman (1989: 52) elaborates in his book, *Modernity and the Holocaust*:

> 'By the very fact of their territorial dispersion and ubiquity, the Jews were an international nation, a non-national nation. Everywhere, they served as a constant reminder of the relativity and limits of individual self-identity and communal interest, which

the criterion of nationhood was meant to determine with absolute and final authority. Inside every nation, they were the "enemy inside". The boundaries of the nation were too narrow to define them; the horizons of national tradition were too short to see through their identity. *The Jews were not just unlike any other nation; they were also unlike any other foreigners.* In short, they undermined the very difference between hosts and guests, the native and the foreign. And as nationhood became the paramount basis of group self-constitution, they came to undermine the most basic of differences: the difference between "us" and "them". Jews were flexible and adaptable; an empty vehicle, ready to be filled with whatever despicable load "them" were charged of carrying.'

In a *'world tightly packed with nations and nation-states'*, *'the non-national void'* that the Jews represented was detested (Bauman, 1989: 53). The Jews *'were the opacity of the world fighting for clarity, the ambiguity of the world lusting for certainty'* (ibid: 56).

Although the science of 'race' was formally discredited after the Second World War (once the full reality of the Holocaust became known), in actual fact, the credibility of 'racial' science was in decline prior to 1933 (the year that Hitler came to power). Since then, the idea of 'race', without the sanction of science, and even without explicit reference to 'race', has continued as a common-sense ideology (Miles and Brown, 2003).

CONTEMPORARY ANTI-JEWISH RACISM ON THE LEFT

Both in the pre-history to the idea of 'race' and the history of racism, negative representations of the Jews have provided common-sense ideological means for making sense of societal change. With the Enlightenment, representations of the Jews pre-existed to provide 'a natural lightning-rod to divert early discharges of anti-modernist energy': 'the point where formidable powers of money met with social disdain, moral condemnation and aesthetic disgust' (Bauman, 1989: 46). The Jewish Other was, as such, the 'anchor' for anti-capitalist sentiments (ibid: 47). By connecting capitalism to the Jews, it could be damned as 'simultaneously alien, unnatural, inimical, dangerous and ethically repulsive', which is what happened as Jews moved from the margins of life and the ghetto (and the label of *usury*) to life's centre and the streets of urban society (as the personification of *capital*) (Bauman, 1989: 46). It is unsurprising, given the conflation of Jews with money power, that the core ideas of anti-Jewish racism have gained traction across the political spectrum. After all, ideas do not exist in silos; ideas are mobile and settle wherever they seem to make sense. Thus, in the history of modern antisemitism, or anti-Jewish racism, the Jew has been made into an enemy of the Left, 'as a cut-throat capitalist bleeding the workers to death', and of the Right, 'as a free-thinking socialist poisoning [...] hearts and minds' (Cohen, 1988: 17).

Bauman (2000: 225) offers a precise definition of present-day racism against the Jews:

'It seems that in the contemporary world the multi-faceted imagery of Jewry, once drawing inspiration from multiple dimensions of "Jewish incongruity", tends to be tapered down to just one fairly straightforward attribute: that *of a supra-national elite, of invisible power behind all visible powers, of a hidden manager of allegedly spontaneous and uncontrollable, but usually unfortunate and baffling turns of fate.*'

From the non-national nation to the international nation, the idea of the Jews as the enemy within the nation and the enemy beyond the nation, plotting behind the scenes and living off immoral capitalism, is a critical and persistent ideological thread of anti-Jewish racism. The geography of the *wandering Jew* is central: the Jewish Other (who is a threat to the Self) cannot be geographically fixed and located, even when there is a nation state of Jews, since this nation state is judged to be innately territorially hungry and expansive, capable of exceptional global control, and to be the global laboratory and globalisation of the world's ills. As such, the termination of terminus Israel is prescribed. Both before and after Israel, Jews are a betrayal of the nation state and nationalism, and the essence of bad capitalism: from the enemy of the nation state to the enemy nation state, all the while representing the harms of capitalism, colonialism and imperialism. The ideological figure of the wandering Jew connects up three historically repetitive claims: 'the Jew as a kind of *vampire*'; 'the Jew as a *hidden hand* secretly manipulating the course of history to visit death and destruction on the body politic'; and 'the Jew as a *parasite* preying on the host society' (Cohen, 1988: 16). Indeed, as Philip Cohen (1988: 17) puts it, 'as soon as wandering Jews' began 'to put down roots', they became 'even more dangerous'; now 'it is the very tenaciousness of Jewish culture which is the threat'.

In a comparison of Islamophobia and antisemitism, old and new, Pnina Werbner (2013: 451) astutely observes their intersection with the politics of the Palestinian-Israeli conflict:

'We find these concepts and the protagonists who enunciate them entangled with each other in mutual recriminations, invoking a wide concatenation of ambiguous, polysemic, ideological tropes: Zionism, Islamism, racism, colonialism, apartheid, genocide, terrorism, Nazism, orientalism, occidentalism.'

She recognises that extremist actions on both sides of the conflict conjure up the racialised 'archetypal demonic figures' of the Jews as conspiratorial witches and the Palestinians as the Islamic Grand Inquisitor (ibid: 455). 'The witch', Werbner (2013: 455–456) elaborates, 'crystallizes fears of the hidden, disguised, malevolent stranger, of a general breakdown of trust [...] Your neighbour may be a witch who wants to destroy you. He or she is culturally indistinguishable in almost every respect because the witch masquerades as a non-alien.' While: 'the Islamic Grand Inquisitor is not a disguised, assimilated threat as the Jewish "witch" [...] He is upfront, morally superior, openly aggressive, denying promiscuous society and the validity of other cultures' (ibid: 458).

Anti-Jewish racism and anti-Muslim racism are racialisations of prior European representations of Self and Other. Both cannot be fully understood without an understanding of how the idea of 'race' reworked earlier representations in response to changing conditions of existence. In his study of the racialisation of medieval Jews, James Thomas (2010: 1751) explains:

'While the vocabularies of difference may have altered in their rhetorical form – from early medieval descriptions of impurity which could be cured through conversion, to late medieval depictions of essential and corporeal inferiority, to the scientific descriptions of biological impurity – the images of the Jew as black, as threatening, and as a demon to both the Christian spirit and the newly formed nation-state persisted over time. [...] The language of nineteenth-century medical science only transmuted earlier assumptions of innate difference from that of the soul to that of the body, but the socio-political consequences were quite similar.'

The early representation of Islam as violent, hostile and threatening, which peaked during the Crusades, resurfaced – revived and reconfigured – in the post-9/11 racialisation of Muslims. Here, Miles and Brown (2003: 164) suggest, 'an amalgam of nationality ("Arab" or "Pakistani", for example), religion (Islam) and politics (extremism, fundamentalism, terrorism)' comes into play in the contemporary racialisation of the Muslim Other. Similarly, there is a blending of

Israel, Zionism and Jewishness with the idea of a cunning and scheming global network of Jewish capitalist and imperialist power (where the invisible wandering Jew is a threat to corporeal existence and world peace) in the contemporary racialisation of the Jewish Other. Furthermore, both anti-Jewish racism and anti-Muslim racism entail a dynamic of conspiratorial racialisation, which is usefully defined by Reza Zia-Ebrahimi (2018) as an ahistorical and unchanging, psychological and moral essentialisation of a population as 'a monolithic group animated by only one will' (319) that is 'the ultimate enemy out for our destruction' (318). Contemporary anti-Jewish racism on the Left is reflected in the idea of the hidden hand of Zionism that is out to destroy 'Us' and in the representation of Zionism as the ultimate epitome of the insidious harm wrought by global capitalism and imperialism on humanity.

CONCLUSION

> 'For the European, the Other has not been created exclusively in the colonial context. Representations of the Other have taken as their subject not only the populations of Africa, the Asian subcontinent and the Americas, but also the populations of different parts of Europe, as well as inwardly migrant populations, notably from North Africa and the Middle East. Moreover, the Other has been created not only externally to the nation state but also within, notably in the Jewish case. Consequently, debate about the nature and origin of representations of the Other cannot be *confined* to the analysis of European colonialism.' (Miles and Brown, 2003: 51)

This chapter has presented a history which shows the centrality of anti-Jewish racism to racism in general, and the potential and actual overlap of racism and nationalism in general. As such, it should now appear all the more concerning that academic research into 'race' and racism tends to be disconnected from antisemitism, and that the academic Left tends to position Zionism as colonialism and racism to the neglect of also recognising Zionism as a form of nationalism in pursuit of insulation from antisemitism. The tendency of contemporary Anglo-American academic work on 'race' and racism to bypass consideration of anti-Jewish racism can be seen as a consequence of the colonial model of racism. Emerging out of the political struggles of the African-American population in the 1960s, the colonial model places the origins of racism exclusively in the history of slavery and colonialism, and conceptualises racism as the persistence of 'white' structural power and dominance over 'black' people. As I will explain in Chapter Three, the 1960s was significant also for the development of the New Left and the shift of much of the revolutionary Left on the Palestinian-Israeli conflict (after Israel's expansionist victory in the June 1967 war) to hostility to Israel as a national entity. Post-1967, for much of the Left, Palestine has become the global symbolic vanguard of anti-imperialism, anti-colonialism and anti-racism. If the colonial model of racism (emerging out of the 1960s) exiled anti-Jewish racism and platformed Zionism as racism, then (after 1967) the general circulation of anti-Jewish racist ideas gained traction in the leftist milieu and ignited the fire that exhorts Zionism as the evil incarnate of imperialism, colonialism and racism. Crucially, during the 1960s and 1970s, the academy was *the space* for the intersection of the colonial model of racism and this new hostility to Israel. The success of Said's *Orientalism* reflects this. This book was written in response to the Western media portrayal of Arabs in the June 1967 war and was published in 1978 (one year after the election, for the first time, of a right-wing government in Israel). It is to the academic Left's analysis of the Palestinian-Israeli conflict that I now turn, to demonstrate the dangerous fusion of the colonial model of racism with 'the Jewish question'.

Chapter 3

THE ACADEMIC LEFT'S 'JEWISH QUESTION' AND COLONIAL MODEL OF RACISM

'The return of the Jewish question involves a distortion of universalism that sees Jews as *the* problem and demands a solution to this problem. Today this demand focuses on the exclusion of the Jewish nation from world society. Condemning a people is no substitute for political thought, even if it presents itself as resistance to power, speaks the language of universalism and prides itself on its left credentials. The practical question for the left is how to escape the prison house of the Jewish question.' (Fine and Spencer, 2017: 123–124)

'I usually don't like to do this, to sort of single out the Jews – but I think in the case of Israel it's inevitable.' (Pappé, cited in Hussein, 2014: 489)

As Fine and Spencer (2017) explain, anti-Jewish racism on the Left is a betrayal of genuine universalism. It pivots on two faces: an emancipatory face that seeks to include the Other as an equal human being, and a repressive face that singles out the Other as a failure of what is required for membership of humanity. On the one hand, solidarity with the Palestinian people and their struggle for an independent national homeland and meaningful compensation for the refugees of the 1948 war is, and should be, a fundamental part of a movement for political and human emancipation. On the other hand, for much of the Left, the positioning of 'the Palestinian' as the ultimate victim of global ills is a dialectical outcome of the racialisation of 'the Jewish Other' as the ultimate betrayal and harm to the global human collective. Put simply, the Jewish nation state (and the Jews associated with it) have become *the* Other and *the* opprobrium of academic Leftist thought. It is not just the case that the Left does not escape 'the Jewish question', rather, it is obsessed by it.

This chapter critiques the hegemonic academic Left literature on the Palestinian-Israeli conflict that considers nothing less than the dismantlement of Israel proper and a repentant body of Jews as acceptable. This chapter maps and explores the defining themes of this academic terrain: the decisive shift, post-Oslo, to a one-state position that removes the Israeli nation state; the tactical application of an apartheid analogy to increase international opprobrium on Israel; the assessment of Zionism as an especially deplorable racism with an innate drive of ethnic cleansing and genocide, which positions the Jews as the new Nazis; the romanticised, critical accommodation of Palestinian Islamist suicide bombing as an inevitable product of asymmetric warfare and the fault of the Jews themselves; and the pitching of an all-or-nothing global battle of progressive forces against the globalising laboratory of ills created by Israel and Zionism.

Central to the topography of this chapter is the academic approach of postcolonialism and its paradigm of settler-colonialism. Postcolonialism is a critical theory that widens the concept of colonialism to analyse how colonial power operates in the present era, decades after the wave of decolonisation ended the main European colonial empires. Said's (1995) *Orientalism* is a central and foundational influence on this theoretical approach, specifically, his concept of Orientalism as the way in which the East is represented in and by Europe and North America to position the West as its cultural superior (Rogers, Castree and Kitchen, 2013). Orientalism is integrated into postcolonial analysis, including the settler-colonialism paradigm, to reveal the knowledge and power relationship between the coloniser and the colonised:

> 'The important thing was to dignify simple conquest with an idea, to turn the appetite for more geographical space into a theory about the special relationship between geography on the one hand and civilized or uncivilized peoples on the other.' (Said, 1995: 216)

Orientalism, as a racialised Othering of the global East by the global West, is a dualistic cultural schema that operates within an exclusively colonial model of racism. This colonial model of racism, along with 'the Jewish question', manifest in the postcolonial application of a settler-colonialism paradigm to the Palestinian-Israeli conflict, with the consequence that anti-Jewish racism disappears from view as Zionism as racism enters the frame – and not just any kind of racism, but a particularly despicable and dangerous racism. In postcolonial analysis, the Palestinian-Israeli conflict has come to symbolise the epitome of 'colonial-settler versus native' struggle, with Islamism in the camp of allies not foes, and Zionism cast out as 'the universal equivalent of the deficiencies of all nationalism' (Fine and Spencer, 2017: 9).

Prior to critiquing the postcolonial approach to the Palestinian-Israeli conflict, I explain how the academic success of Said's *Orientalism* in the New Left of the late 1960s and 1970s has led to the general displacement of the spirit of Marxism that I resuscitate in Chapter Four to challenge the exclusion of the Jewish collective. Specifically, I suggest that the academic Left consensus on the ideas of *Orientalism* has effectively banished the work of the scholar Maxime Rodinson and his original concept of settler-colonialism vis-à-vis Israel. This, I demonstrate, is a critical loss, since Rodinson's analysis is free from both the colonial model of racism and 'the Jewish question'.

THE LEGACY OF THE NEW LEFT
AND SAID'S *ORIENTALISM*

A weakened labour movement and a discredited Marxist orthodoxy, seen as part of the Old Left, contributed to the formation of the journal *New Left Review* in 1960, which sought to focus on the anti-imperialist movements of the Third World (see: Anderson, 2000). The New Left of the 1960s and 1970s, both in the US and Europe, represented an orientation away from class-centred politics towards activism linked to broader protest movements and mass politics, with its proponents ideologically drawing from, notably, Debray, Fanon, Guevara, and Mao (Buhle, 1991; Cohen, 2004). This New Left was motivated by the national liberation struggle of the Viet Cong in North Vietnam, the national revolutions of Cuba and Algeria, and, as a consequence of the June 1967 Arab–Israeli war, the Palestinian plight:

'The Israeli victory in the 1967 war and subsequent settlement of occupied Arab territories [...] brought the younger generation of Western Marxists, the Trotskyist or Maoist "new left", to an extreme anti-Israeli position. Israel, which from 1967 also developed close relations with the US, was condemned as racist, the oppressor of the Palestinians and the main progenitor of imperialism and colonialism in the Middle East.' (Golan 2001: 129)

Prior to 1967, general public opinion in the West, including on the Left, regarded Israel as a civilised country amid backward, barbaric masses who desired its annihilation (Rodinson, 1968, 1983). Post-1967, Israel's right to exist as a nation state was called into question by a new generation of Maoists, Trotskyists and New Leftists (Bassi, 2011; Cohen, 2004; Crooke, 2002; Golan, 2001). The 'militant anti-imperialism' of the 1968 Palestine Liberation Organisation's Charter, including its call for a democratic secular Palestinian state in all of former British Mandate Palestine, situated the Palestinian cause 'at the forefront' of the New Left's broad revolutionary politics (Hassan, 2001: 64).

Pro-Israel demonstrations in the run up to the 1967 war had a profound influence on Said, who states, '1967 in New York, was probably the most shattering experience in my life, because I was surrounded on all sides by people who identified with the Israeli victors' (Said, cited in Katz and Smith, 2003: 645). The portrayal of Arabs in the Western media during this time motivated his writing of *Orientalism* (Katz and Smith, 2003). Although the movements of the New Left ebbed by the end of the 1970s, a number of its student participants took up junior faculty positions and academic agendas shifted to the political left. In this context, 'Said's *Orientalism*', published in 1978, and one year after the election, for the first time, of a right-wing Israeli government, 'far from bucking convention, actually rode the crest of this immensely successful academic uprising' (Kramer, 2001: 31). One of the book's lasting effects, as seen in the development of postcolonial studies, has been to shift the meaning of the term Orientalism away from a descriptor of Oriental Studies to that of 'a Western style for dominating, restructuring, and having authority over the Orient' (Said, 1995: 3). Orientalism has subsequently become a slur to tarnish (wholesale) Orientalist scholars and other supposedly guilty intellectuals like Karl Marx. The legacy of Said's *Orientalism* for academic research on the Palestinian-Israeli conflict is spelt out by Professor Emerita of History at the University of California, Los Angeles, Nikki Keddie (cited in Gallagher, 1996: 144–145):

> 'I think that there has been a tendency in the Middle East field to adopt the word "orientalism" as a generalized swear-word essentially referring to people who take the "wrong" position on the Arab-Israeli dispute or to people who are judged too "conservative". It has nothing to do with whether they are good or not good

in their disciplines. So "orientalism" for many people is a word that substitutes for thought and enables people to dismiss certain scholars and their works. I think that is too bad. It may not have been what Edward Said meant at all, but the term has become a kind of slogan.'

For Said, the Palestinians were the latest victims of Orientalism and the West's intolerance of Arabs, Muslims and the East. He states:

'Israel was a device for holding Islam – later the Soviet Union, or communism – at bay. Zionism and Israel were associated with liberalism, with freedom and democracy, with knowledge and light, with what "we" understand and fight for. By contrast, Zionism's enemies were simply a twentieth-century version of the alien spirit of Oriental despotism, sensuality, ignorance, and similar forms of backwardness.' (Said, 1980: 29, cited in Ashcroft and Ahluwalia, 2001: 120)

A key aim of the postcolonial academic Left is thus 'to put an end to the recurrent and insidious "demonisation" of the Palestinians in the Israeli media and public mind', since this 'form of Orientalism is pernicious and has poisoned the perception of the Palestinian struggle in Israel and across the North Atlantic world' (Falah, 2001: 136). Rodinson, who is consequently damned on two counts as an Orientalist and a Marxist, is nevertheless acknowledged by Said (1995) in *Orientalism* for his 'extraordinary achievements' (266) and as someone who has proved 'perfectly capable of freeing [himself] from the old ideological straitjacket' of the Orientalist discipline (326). A significant consequence, however, of the popularity of Said's *Orientalism* in academic thought is that Rodinson's work has been effectively lost or dismissed, along with his exemplar of how to criticise the colonial and racist dimensions of Israel free from both anti-Jewish racism and the requisite to eliminate this nation state.

In *Confronting Antisemitism on the Left*, Daniel Randall (2021) identifies and explores three historical strands to antisemitism on the Left: one, primitive antisemitism, in which capitalism is viewed and problematised as innately Jewish; two, the conspiracy theories of the so-called Communist bloc, from especially the 1950s, against a supposed secret cabal of cosmopolitan and Zionist Jews; and three, a Stalinist anti-Zionism that frames Zionism (Jewish nationalism) as a transcendent force of imperialism, colonialism and racism. It seems likely that this Stalinist anti-Zionism shaped the general approach of the New Left to the Palestinian-Israeli conflict after 1967. Indeed, Rodinson cautions that Said's *Orientalism* is 'a polemic against orientalism written in a style that was a bit Stalinist' (1980, cited in Kramer, 2001: 38), that is, in its dual camp delineation of the world into 'adversaries' and 'allies', which here translates into 'colonial-settler' versus 'native', 'white' versus 'black' and 'harmful Jew' versus 'Palestinian victim'. The problem with left-wing dual camp politics is that it fetishises and inverts the bourgeois dual camp of major imperialist powers who present geopolitical moments as a moral choice of 'civilisation' versus 'barbarism' and 'good' versus 'evil', and, in this process, it substitutes consideration of the *politics* of particular camps for the principle of my enemy's enemy is my friend. The task, instead, is to construct an alternative and independent force of political thought and action: by and for the interests of the working class, trade unionists, secularists, anti-racists, feminists, queer activists, and so on, which can transcend socially constructed differences amid humankind, such as nationality, religion and 'race'.

REPENT OR BE DOOMED

The failure of the Oslo Accords to create an independent Palestinian nation state, along with Said's (1999) shift from advocating a two-state to one-state solution, have fuelled a revival of a settler-colonialism paradigm in postcolonial academic literature. The settler-colonialism paradigm situates the Palestinian-Israeli conflict in 1948 not 1967, with the *al Nakba* representing a continuation of colonisation to the present. Furthermore, this paradigm views the conflict as settler versus native, regards both the peace process and the two-state solution as legitimising and cementing colonialism, and concludes a resolution to the conflict as decolonisation in the form of one-state in historic Palestine for the entire Palestinian constituency (that can accommodate repentant Jews). In this discourse, the Oslo peace process is regarded as a fake 'peace process' and, in fact, opportunism by Israel for 'conquest through the pursuit of colonization on an unprecedented scale' (Mansour, 2001: 86) that 'simply re-packaged the occupation' (Said, 2001: 2) with the 'function […] to cage Palestinians in a remnant of their own lands' (Said, 2000: 6). Consequently, post-Oslo, a critical mass of academics previously calling for a two-state solution have turned to a one-state position as a logical outcome of the settler-colonialism paradigm. Various formats of a one-state solution now make up the majority of opinion in published academic research on the Palestinian-Israeli conflict. The basic argument of one-state advocates is that the conditions on the ground for a two-state solution no longer exist:

> 'There are too many settlements, too many Jewish settlers, and too many Palestinians, and they all live together, albeit separated by barbed wire and pass laws. Whatever the "road map" says, the real map is the one on the ground, and that, as Israelis say, reflects facts. […] The time has come to think the unthinkable. The two-state solution – the core of the Oslo process and the present "road map" – is probably already doomed.' (Judt, 2003)

Virginia Tilley (2005: 1) declares, 'only one state can viably exist in the land of historic Palestine between the Mediterranean and the

Jordan River'. Moreover, a gestalt shift is needed, Ian Lustick (2019, 2021) argues, to see that the two-state solution can no longer happen because of the one-state reality from the river to the sea. Taking a steer from debates in the 1980s in response to South African apartheid, Lustick (2021) states that the real question in the United States and Europe for the next ten to thirty years is sanctions against Israel.

While the settler-colonialism paradigm potentially opens up wide-ranging sites of comparison, Rachel Busbridge (2018: 97) observes that in actuality 'there is a particularly strong emphasis' on white European settler-colonialism, vis-à-vis Americas, Australasia and Israel-Palestine, to the omission of other settler-colonial relationships like Russia-Chechnya or China-Tibet. An academic understanding of the world through a colonial model of racism, including Orientalism, explains this phenomenon: the story of the Palestinian-Israeli conflict fits (or rather is made to fit) a dualistic racialised schema. 'The story here is a simple story,' Pappé (2007) tells us, it is 'a story of white people who were persecuted in Europe and who drove away the black people who used to live here.' He continues, the 'villains', presenting themselves as 'heroes', are 'the Israelis': 'They were and are servants of the bureaucracy of evil. They come quite innocent into the system but only the very few among them do not succumb to its *raison d'etre* and modus operandi' (Pappé, 2013: 350).

Here, explicitly, 'white' Jews and 'black' Palestinians are racialised into culturally essentialist groups, with the Jews signified as the submissive lackies of evil. The task, Pappé (2007) insists, is to expose, isolate and revoke Israel as 'a pariah state'. The takeaway message to Jews associated with Israel and Zionism is, repent or be doomed.

In essence, the settler-colonialism paradigm is 'a repackaging' (Busbridge, 2018: 98) and 'a new dictionary' (Pappé, 2013: 350) of the Palestinian-Israeli conflict intended to make it more relatable to New World white settler societies and to accordingly grow the internationalisation of Palestinian solidarity through the language of indigenous and native, anti-colonial politics (Busbridge, 2018). In this context, and as part of the global activist movement, Boycott, Divestment and Sanctions, this academic body of literature provides the intellectual authority to a 'strategy of "South-Africanising" the Palestinian-Israeli conflict' (Hussein, 2015: 541). South African apartheid is openly considered the ideal candidate for comparison to Zionist Israel for two key reasons: one, as an example of settler-colonialism, it ended; two, 'the crime of apartheid is a familiar concept' for rousing sympathy for the Palestinians, notably, among both 'African Americans in the US that are surprisingly pro-Zionist' and 'progressive Jews' (Pappé, cited in Hussein, 2014: 491). There is, implicitly, I would suggest, one more reason: South African apartheid is seen to epitomise the depravity of rich white people doing bad things to poor black people, so if this well-known story of moral damnation can be translated to the Palestinian-Israeli conflict, a similar moral perdition of Israel could be achieved.

South African apartheid operated through a racialised structure of a narrow caste exploiting the labour-power of a majority population. This is not a racialised class structure that is present in Israel. However, the 2002 Rome Statute of the International Criminal Court, alongside the 1973 United Nations General Assembly's International Convention on the Suppression and Punishment of the Crime of Apartheid, define apartheid as the institutionalised and regime-maintaining, systematic domination and oppression of one 'racial' group over another 'racial' group. It is this broader definition of apartheid which is mobilised to depict Zionist Israel as an apartheid racist state. Myanmar's ethnic cleansing and segregation of the Rohingya population (see: Mahmood, Wroe, Fuller, and Leaning, 2016; Ullah, 2016), and China's persecution of the Uyghur-majority population in the state of Xinjiang through the internment of an estimated one million Uyghurs in re-education camps (see: Caksu, 2020; Smith Finley, 2021), would also fall under this definition of apartheid.

However, it is Israel that is exceptionalised as apartheid in this body of leftist academic literature and by the wider Boycott, Divestment and Sanctions movement.

The intention of the settler-colonialism paradigm is to make the Palestinian-Israeli conflict more relatable in order to yield greater support for the Palestinian plight and greater hostility towards Israel; however, its application is not intended to de-exceptionalise the conflict. As one of the main theoreticians of the settler-colonialism paradigm, Lorenzo Veracini (2019: 569–570) concedes, regardless of the comparative framework that potentially covers 'a vast array of locales, a significant part of [the] output has been about Palestine'; moreover, 'appraising Zionism and settler colonialism in the same interpretive framework does not amount to saying that Zionism is *just like* other settler colonialisms'. This chapter proceeds to illustrate how Zionist Israel is considered both the exceptional outlier of a decolonisation era and an exceptional forerunner of colonialism, imperialism and racism.

ZIONISM AS A COLONIALISM OF ETHNIC CLEANSING TO GENOCIDE

In the postcolonialism framework, the logic of elimination or containment of natives from or on their territory and their replacement with settlers is seen to shape the power structure of settler-colonialism, in contrast to the logic of exploitation of colonialised labour that is central to colonialism's power relationship (see: Wolfe, 2006; Veracini, 2019). Settler-colonialism's elimination drive is referred to as ethnic cleansing. As a spatial cleansing of an indigenous group from its territory, Neve Gordon and Moriel Ram (2016: 21) trace the origin of the term to the Serbo-Croatian phrase '*etnicko ci scenje*' employed by commentators during the 1992–1995 war and breakup of Yugoslavia. They note, 'a growing debate on the exact characterization of ethnic cleansing and its relation to other forms of systematic violence such as genocide, ethnocide or politicide' (ibid: 22). Nevertheless, a trajectory of argument exists that Zionism's relentless quest for ethnic cleansing is an 'indicator' of the potential genocide to come: 'As Palestinians become more and more dispensable, Gaza and the West Bank become less and less like Bantustans and more and more like reservations (or, for that matter, like the Warsaw Ghetto). Porous borders do not offer a way out' (Wolfe, 2006: 403–404).

This looming genocide is here specified as a genocide of the victim turned persecutor: the Jews of the Warsaw Ghetto now trap Palestinians in their own Warsaw Ghetto. Wolfe (2006: 401) remarks, given 'Zionism's chronic addition to territorial expansion', 'it is hardly surprising that a nation that has driven so many of its original inhabitants into the sand should express an abiding fear of itself being driven into the sea'. Wolfe's presentation of Jewish nationalism is as an essentialised Zionist monster who is chronically destructive: this monster will never stop its ethnic cleansing, up to and including genocide; what's more, those forces wishing to drive Jews into the sea are of this monster's own making. On early Zionism's drive to eliminate Palestinians from their territory, Wolfe (2006: 396) spells out an irony that 'the feminized, finance-oriented (or, for that matter, wandering) Jew of European anti-Semitism' asserted 'an aggressively masculine agricultural self-identification in Palestine'. There is no reason to identify any irony unless Wolfe's intention is to take something away from Jewish experience of European antisemitism and the Holocaust as the reality that drove significant numbers of Jews out of Europe to seek refuge and home in Palestine. This narrative of the past victim of racism turned the contemporary racist persecutor negates the past horror of antisemitism by making more morally deplorable the racist crimes of the modern-day Jew.

Returning to the spectre of an essentialised and essentially hungry Zionist monster, the Zionist intention to expel on a mass scale,

Gabriel Piterberg (2001: 34) insists, was 'inherent' long before 1948, with, Pappé (2006: 9) elaborates, the outcome of the 1948 war 'the result of long and meticulous planning' by the Zionists to ethnically cleanse Palestinians from Palestinian land. As such, Pappé (2006) demands, the paradigm of war must be replaced with a paradigm of ethnic cleansing on 1948 to redress the erasure of this Zionist crime from global memory and conscience, which international law would today recognise as a crime against humanity. Finkelstein (2002) claims that 1948 was exploited by the Zionists in a manner comparable to the Serbian ethnic cleansing in Kosovo during the 1999 NATO intervention. But unless Finkelstein is ignorant of the evidence of both Serbian ethnic cleansing and genocide in Kosovo at this time (see: Ronayne, 2004), he deliberately and provocatively blurs the line between ethnic cleansing and genocide. In general, there is an absence of consideration in this literature of Zionism's origins as a nationalist aspiration and movement that developed amid violent antisemitic conditions in central and eastern Europe (Golan, 2001) and of early Zionist settlement as both a colonial and an anti-colonial undertaking, given the murderous conditions facing Jews in Europe and their denial of emigration elsewhere in the West (Yiftachel, 2002). Zionism as a colonialism of ethnic cleansing is not afforded the reality of early Zionism as a 'colonialism of the displaced' or a '*colonialism of ethnic survival*' (Yiftachel, 2002: 224–225). Instead, early to late Zionism is made into the same unchanging, monolithic beast: intent on ethnic cleansing to the point of genocide.

Mapping a continuum of pre-1948 to present-day Zionist enclaving and exclaving of Palestinian territory, Ghazi Falah (2003) conceptualises a 'social and spatial apartheid' (185) consolidated through the employment of 'racist national ideas, often in "socialist" guise' (187), and 'a practice that today elsewhere would be called ethnic cleansing' (206). He warns, 'nothing but full annihilation of the Palestinian-Arab people is the ultimate covert goal' (Falah, 2003: 182). Developing this theme, 'From Urbicide to Genocide?' is the rhetorical question posed by Stephen Graham (2002: 647) on everyday life in the Occupied Territories, as the Zionist state responds to the Palestinian demographic threat to its existence by bulldozer. He uses the example of an ultra-right political and military Israeli leader to reveal that:

> 'the corporeal "body-as-state" metaphors of "cancers" and "orderly bodies" [...] regularly employ[ed] to describe Arab settlements are virtually search-and-replace copies of Hitler's metaphorical depictions of Jewish ghettos in *Mein Kampf*. From countless examples in history, it is obvious that from such metaphors genocides can grow. The Jewish people should be the last to need lessons on how quickly this can happen.' (Graham, 2002: 647–648)

Graham blends the exceptional into the everyday to expose an exceptionally harmful Israeli Jewish reality of normalised urbicide-to-genocide. He achieves this claim by conflating a Jewish ultra-rightist into the Jewish people, who should know better than any other group of people to not become the new fascists faithfully putting into practice Hitler's *Mein Kampf*. Drawing on the philosopher Giorgio Agamben, Derek Gregory (2004a: 133) points to the 'hideous objective' of the Israeli government 'to reduce *homo sacer* to the abject despair of *der Muselmann*'. This, he stresses, is 'truly shocking' because '*[d]er Muselmann* is a figure from the Nazi concentration camps [...] who was reduced to mere survival' (ibid: 133). To note the parallels here, Gregory (2004a: 133–134) states, 'is *not* to be anti-Semitic'. However, once again, this past victim turned contemporary persecutor narrative lessens the moral depravity of German fascism and the Holocaust by identifying a greater moral depravity in the Jews themselves advancing this genocidal trajectory. Furthermore, reference to Nazi Germany and the Holocaust is not made to discuss how genocidal antisemitism was a critical factor of early Zionism and the realisation of the nation state of Israel. Instead, this reference is consciously employed to spell out how Zionism is a particularly destructive colonialism comparable to genocidal Nazi fascism.

'The Zionist dream of uniting the diaspora in a Jewish state was by its very nature a colonial project' (Gregory, 2004a: 78), but not just any settler-colonial project, it is argued, since Zionism is particularly harmful. Israel's legal foundations – specifically, the Law of Return, the Nationality Law, the status of present-absentees, and the prevention of the right of return for Palestinian refugees – are seen as a pre-1948 to present-day quest for national and racial purity which, Said (1985: 41) asserts, is 'tantamount to organized discrimination or persecution: the examples of Nazi Germany and South Africa argue the force of such a judgment with considerable authority in today's world'.

The post-1967 era is seen to have solidified the unique link between Zionist Israel, the US Zionist lobby and US imperialism: particularly in 'the unprecedented munificence that the United States bestows on Israel', that is, 'the moral equivalent of a blank cheque to do what it likes' (Said, 1986: 79). Together with the power of the Zionist lobby, the concept of Orientalism (as a form of racism) is used to explain the impunity of Israel's crimes in the West:

'The pain of the Palestinian people is something not easily translatable on our Western television screens. These brown people look different to "us" [...] Anti-Arab racism and Islamophobia, the acceptable forms of bigotry in our times, go a long way toward giving subsequent Israeli governments a green light to continue their practices.' (Jamoul, 2004: 592)

Given the continued drive of ethnic cleansing from pre-1948 to the present-day, Gregory (2004a: 94) reasons, 'can there be any doubt that this was – and remains – colonialism of the most repressive kind?' Falah (2001: 135) similarly declares that the contemporary 'knee-jerk militarism that pervades Israeli-Jewish society has no parallel anywhere in the democratic world', consolidating the theory that 'a kind of "democratic fascism" has entrenched itself within the Israeli polity – and the consciousness of many of its citizens'. Indeed, problematically, for 'many on the Israeli Left [...] the key date is 1967, when Israel advanced again', not 1948 (Gregory, 2004b: 602). Jews who associate with Jewish nationalism, the nation state of Israel, and early Zionism's role in ethnic survival, are themselves (in all of their social, cultural, economic, and political complexities and tensions) racialised as driven by an inherent tendency towards destruction. 'The Jewish question' reaches a crescendo here, as individual Jews are absorbed into the negatively racialised body of Zionism, which is an unprecedented, detrimental power on the global stage. Conjuring up the two exceptional racist and fascist regimes of the twentieth century, Lina Jamoul (2004: 592) concludes: 'Israel conducts its own holocaust, creating a twenty-first century Apartheid'. The takeaway conclusion to 'the Jewish question' is that the Jewish nation state and its related Jews are a unique threat to the world and must be stopped.

Criticism of the Israeli state and military is here exceptionalised through 'the Jewish question': what is to be done with a nation state guilty of an ethnic cleansing and racism on par with South African apartheid and Nazi Germany; what is to be done with Zionism's national racism that has even gone so far as to historically present itself as socialist; what is to be done with so-called left-wing Jews who fail to see the origins of the Palestinian-Israeli conflict in 1948, not 1967; what is to be done with the Jews who have failed to learn their lesson from the Holocaust; what is to be done with an innate drive within Zionism and Zionist Jews to ethnically cleanse to the destiny of genocide. The conclusion to 'the Jewish question': undo Israel.

The spatial and temporal aspects of this racialised construction of Zionism are notable: Zionism is spatially *fluid* – with a territorial hunger and global reach that knows no bounds – and temporally *frozen*. On the temporal aspect, Joyce Dalsheim (2013: 32) astutely identifies a contradictory anachronism employed in the Palestinian-Israeli conflict: 'Some "people out of time" arouse anger, revulsion and condemnation, while others inspire sympathy.'

Jewish territorial nationalism and Jewish settlers in the Occupied Territories are 'out of time', provoking denunciation; Palestinians as a national group cannot advance toward national liberation as they are trapped in a settler-colonialism that is 'out of time', provoking pity (Dalsheim, 2013). The following comment by Jamoul (2004: 593) demonstrates this anachronism, with a hint of romanticisation for a vintage struggle in the contemporary world: 'In a so-called twenty-first century postmodern world, where in the northern hemisphere history is declared dead, the Palestinians find themselves engaged in the old-fashioned battles of the nineteenth and twentieth centuries – the battle against colonialism, the struggle for national self-determination and independent statehood.'

The answer to 'the Jewish question' presents here as the Jews must give up their national home to belong to civilisation. What is interesting is that Palestinians too are racialised: Palestinians need to realise their national home to at last belong to civilisation. The stage is cast in postcolonial analysis for the heroes and the villains, with no room for nuance. For example, on the one hand, there is no intellectual room to consider the Jewish settler who lives in the Occupied Territories because they cannot afford housing inside Israel and who is open to co-existing with Palestinians in a liberated Palestine alongside Israel (see Dalsheim, 2011). On the other hand, there is no inclination to critically assess the reactionary politics and military tactics of Islamist resistance. 'The Jewish question' in this literature outcasts Jews from the universal human collective, unless penitent of the sins of Israel and Zionism, and romanticise those in defiance of such Jews. The colonisers – Israeli Jews and Jewish settlers – are deemed to require 'a radical psychological shift and deconstruction of a certain narcissism based on illusory identity', because 'colonialism [...] creates "monsters" out of men' (Dalsheim, 2013: 50). The colonised Palestinian Islamists are 'subalterns with legitimate reasons for rebelling against Israeli oppression' – 'we may abhor their use of violence, but guess that it might disappear were they liberated' (Dalsheim, 2013: 33). Both actors are essentialised and given innately negative (in the case of the Jews) or innately positive (in the case of the Palestinians) consequences. It is from the postcolonial casting of the 'Zionist monster' to the 'Islamist subaltern' that I now turn, for one cannot understand the dialectical racialisation of one without the other.

ISLAMIST RESISTANCE

Palestinian suicide bombings (including attacks that were averted) increased during the Second Intifada (2000–2005) but have declined significantly over recent years. It is nonetheless revealing and relevant how this 'resistance to Israel' has been framed. There is a tendency on the academic Left to understand the phenomenon of Palestinian suicide bombing against Israeli Jews as simply a product of Israeli subjugation, and to regard the Palestinian Islamist organisation of Hamas as part of the global decolonisation movement against Israel and Zionism. There is also a romanticisation of the ability of the Palestinian suicide bomber, as the Palestinian David, to hit back against the Zionist Goliath. This is an ahistorical and de-contextual approach to Islamism, which fits into an Orientalism framework and colonial model of racism, and enables the argument that: 'the accusation that all Palestinians are suicide bombers is racist, but those who have become suicide bombers are actually a product of Israeli racist repression'. While it is the case that the essentialisation of Palestinians as terrorists is racist, attributing the source of Palestinian suicide bombing to Zionist settler-colonial racism carries the problematic implication that the act of Palestinian suicide bombing is an anti-racist one. Demonstrating this, through a conflation of Zionism with Orientalism (i.e., Zionism as racism), Joseph Massad (cited in Hussein, 2015: 537) states, 'the attempt to depict Hamas through an Orientalist Zionist or even secular chauvinist lens as some unchanging Islamist chauvinist group is not only untrue, but anti-Islamist.' In other words, Massad claims that criticism of Islamism is racist and pro-Zionist. In a postcolonial academic critique of Orientalist racism – a racism which is seen to falsely pitch the Palestinian-Israeli conflict as symmetrical, and to falsely blame the Palestinian terrorist for the conflict's violence – it is spelt out that this is an asymmetric conflict, in which the actual Palestinian suicide bomber, however misguided, is punching up and is thus on the right side of history. The anti-Jewish racism that is core to Islamist ideology and practice is absent from discussion.

The successful, widely cited academic of nationalism and racism, Ghassan Hage, expresses, in an influential paper titled, '"Comes a Time We Are All Enthusiasm": Understanding Palestinian Suicide Bombers in Times of Exighophobia' (2003), his unease with the demand to absolutely condemn Palestinian suicide bombers. He suggests, instead, an absolute condemnation of the conditions that create Palestinian suicide bombers. Drawing on Hage's (2003) work, suicide bombing attacks, Gregory (2004a: 105) states, are 'the product of a profound, desperate anger born out of the sustained and asymmetric violence' of Israeli occupation. In the context of the Oslo peace process, Walid Khalidi (2003: 56) explains, Palestinian suicide bombings are an 'inevitable reaction' to 'provocative Israeli policy' and asymmetric warfare. Gregory (2004a: 105) continues, these attacks are an inevitable outlet to 'the continuous accumulation of the countless hurts and humiliations of occupation'. Similarly, Falah (2004) argues, Israeli subjugation of Palestinians in the West Bank and Gaza Strip is tantamount to 'suffocation' (597) and 'existential asphyxiation' (600), which drives some 'to that awful brink [...] where they [...] sacrifice their very body as a weapon in the struggle' (600). The simple explanation here is that racist colonial Zionism creates anti-colonial Islamist blowback, so, when Israeli Jews are killed or maimed by Palestinian suicide bombers, this is a situation of their (the Jews) own making, because the suicide bombers were forced to do so. The question of human agency, and the politics guiding human agency, is superseded by a deterministic set of conditions of existence. The Palestinian suicide bomber is part of the history of anti-colonial struggle, Hage (2003: 68) remarks, in which there has always been violent resistance against the coloniser: the Palestinian suicide bomber acts 'against the Jewish colonizers of Palestine and their descendants in Israel and the occupied territories, who are seen as continuing the colonial enterprise'. The politics of Islamism that wins over a segment of human agency is not analysed; what takes the place of such analysis is the positioning of suicide bombers as the inevitable products of asymmetric warfare and the need to strike back. We are simply told, the Palestinians are left with 'understandable desperation' in the form of 'suicide bombs' (Pappé, 2013: 349), and that 'the temptation to turn suicidal is not so impossible to comprehend' (Khalidi, 2003: 57). Turning suicidal, it is worth noting here, is clearly not the same as turning oneself into a suicide bomb.

The romanticisation of a Palestinian David against the Zionist Goliath is evident in the idea that the Palestinian suicide bombers are capable of realising the necessity to resist regardless of the absence of military means to do so. This romanticisation is fuelled by a colonial model of racism that frames suicide bombers as a product of racism and a part of anti-racist resistance. Illustrating this, Hage (2003: 73–74) draws on an essay by Michael Neumann, in which Neumann (2002) states:

> 'Like the [Native American] Indians, the Palestinians have not the slightest chance of injuring, let alone defeating Israel through conventional military tactics. Like the whites, every single Israeli

Jew, down to and including the children, are instruments wielded against the Palestinian people. The Palestinians don't set out to massacre children [...] They merely hit soft targets, and this sometimes involves the death of children. But, like anyone, they will kill children to prevent the destruction of their society'.

Palestinian suicide bombers 'disrupt the ability of the colonizers to consolidate a "normal peaceful life" inside the colonial settler state of Israel', Hage (2003: 68) observes. This statement implies that 'normal peaceful life' is not something that Israeli Jews deserve. In a 'war of (asymmetric) urbicide', Graham (2002: 648) affirms, 'Palestinians have their own weapon against the modern urban life of the Israelis': 'Untraceable and unstoppable, bypassing fences, checkpoints and targeted assassinations alike, and driven by despair, vengeance and religious certitude, the suicide bomb continues to deny Israelis *their* modernity, *their* cities, *their* freedom.'

This apparent tract of admiration for the suicide bomber who beats Zionist modern warfare and colonial control likewise works on the premise that Israeli Jews do not deserve 'their' modernity, 'their' cities, and 'their' freedom, because these things are not theirs and were not theirs to take. Jamoul (2004: 592–593) also demonstrates a respect for the suicide bomber who finds a means to damage the Other who causes them suffering, in conditions where such means are scarce:

'What has to be recognised is that this is one of the few weapons left to people who have no functioning police force, let alone an army. What is happening in Israel/Palestine is a war, and people will use whatever weapons they have, including their bodies, to fend for themselves and inflict damage on those they see responsible for their suffering. The body you have tried to put a curfew on, detain, beat, imprison, starve into subservience; it will eventually, literally blow up in your face.'

Here Jamoul attributes full cause for Palestinian suicide bombing to Zionist repression. She appears to have no problem stating that this is blowback which literally blows up in the face of the Israeli Jew.

Palestinian suicide bombers are a source of inspiration and hope in the Arab world, Hage (2003: 74) professes, who provide 'a sign of life': 'for what better sign of life is there, in such violent conditions, than the capacity to hurt despite the greater capacity of the other to hurt you'. He elaborates, amid a physical existence of despair and 'social death' (78), the suicide bomber represents 'symbolic existence' through 'suicidal capital' (80) and a chance for young men to make something of themselves (Hage, 2003). 'Channeling [...] colonial affect', suicide bombing transforms 'stoked violence born out of colonial impotence into anticolonial potency' (Hage 2003: 83). This is an astounding academic perspective on Palestinian Islamist suicide bombing, which fails to analyse the politics of Islamism underlying this act of death and destruction against Israeli Jews. While Hage (2003) concludes on the necessity to see evil in conditions of existence not human beings, this principle is not one he extends to Israeli Jews, perhaps because the Jews are seen to create the evil conditions in the first place.

On Hage's (2003: 74) notion that the Palestinian Islamist suicide bomber represents 'a sign of life', I am reminded of the work of the humanistic Marxist philosopher and psychoanalyst Erich Fromm on biophilia and necrophilia: the contradictory tendencies for love of life and love of death. Fromm considers biophilia, the love of life, as an innate tendency in all living beings to preserve life and to fight death, and to integrate and to unite. Crucially, however, it is conditions of existence that shape (but, importantly, not determine) human beings and the potentiality of biophilia to thrive:

> 'Creation and destruction, love and hate, are not two instincts which exist independently. They are both answers to the same

need for transcendence, and the will to destroy must rise when the will to create cannot be satisfied. However, the satisfaction of the need to create leads to happiness; destructiveness to suffering, most of all, for the destroyer himself [*sic*].' (Fromm, 1956: 38)

Hage's (2003) claim that, amid violence, there is no better sign of life than the Palestinian suicide bomber's capability to hurt Israeli Jews, despite the Israelis' greater ability to hurt the Palestinians, is not a politics of biophilia but one of necrophilia. Fromm (1964: 48) explains that those in whom the necrophiliac tendency comes to dominate: 'will slowly kill the biophilic side in themselves; usually they are not aware of their death-loving orientation; they will harden their hearts; they will act in such a way that their love of death seems to be the logical and rational response to what they experience.'

What Hage (2003) misses is the tragedy of the necrophiliac act of the suicide bomber: after all, 'if he [*sic*] believes that he dwells in the land of life when in reality he lives in the land of death, he is lost to life since he has no chance to return' (Fromm, 1964: 48).

A 'Lawrence of academia syndrome' captures well the inverted Orientalism (of the Zionist monster versus the Palestinian Islamist subaltern) of many on the postcolonial academic Left: 'an incredibly myopic paternalism' in the defence of Islamism and its use of suicide bombing (Munson, 1996: 103). In a study of how the Muslim world perceives the Muslim-Jewish relationship since the formation of Israel in 1948, Suha Taji-Farouki (2004: 327) observes how 'the Jewish question' has come to assume 'a profound existential significance' in 'the heart of Arab-Muslim existence', with two key aspects.

The first aspect entails:

'a systematic and detailed exposition of what is construed in an abstract sense as the Jews' *innate* evil and vices. [...] Their in-built hostility to the interests of non-Jews is underlined, and their suffering across the ages are held to be the inevitable fruit of their own character and conduct.' (Taji-Farouki, 2004: 328–329)

The essentialised evil Jew is 'an irredeemable destructive agent' conflated with the Crusades, Freemasonry, Satanism, homosexuality, America, and the West (Webman, 2015: 289). Featuring prominently in the work of the foundational Islamist theorist Sayyid Qutb, the Jew is seen to represent the ills of the Islamic world and a global Jewish conspiracy to destroy Islam, including the tactic of Zionist infiltration of Muslim societies to turn Muslims themselves into traitors (Munson, 1996; Taji-Farouki, 2004; Webman, 2015). Accordingly, the insult 'dirty Jew' is directed not just against Jews but against Muslims also who are considered to contradict the values of Islam (Webman, 2015). Interestingly, when the *Protocols of the Elders of Zion* features, it is as a 'support text' (Taji-Farouki, 2004: 336).

The second aspect of how the Muslim world perceives the Muslim-Jewish relationship is the belief that the Jewish nation state is an aberration that must be destroyed:

'Israel is [...] regarded as a "cancer" or "poisoned dagger" plunged into the heart of the Muslim world. It is an inherently expansionist state, and constitutes an existential danger to the Muslim world. Occasionally, the Western powers are themselves construed as victims of the international Zionist conspiracy, used to serve Zionist goals, and Israel is described as an enemy of humanity as a whole.' (Taji-Farouki, 2004: 340)

Palestine is central here – evoking an unrivalled 'intensity of Muslim sentiment' (Taji-Farouki, 2004: 350). The success of Zionism is seen as the failure of Muslim leaders. As such, while for many Islamists, 'a finite truce with the usurper-occupier based on non-recognition of its right to the land might be entertained for tactical purposes', a permanent restoration of friendly relations is considered impermissible (ibid: 341). Islamist discourse conjures up the history of the Crusades to argue the necessity for every Muslim to fight for Palestine right up to the expulsion of the very last Jew, '"even if", according to one Islamist movement [Hizb al-Tahrir], "this costs them millions of martyrs, and takes centuries"' (Taji-Farouki, 2004: 341).

The portrayal of Palestinian Islamism as anti-colonial and anti-racist resistance against Israel ignores the anti-Jewish racism of Islamist politics (which has a wide and popular base) and fails to consider the threat that Islamism poses to people who identify as Jewish and who are labelled as impious Muslims. Presenting 'suicide bombings' as 'a minimal form of violence in Palestine today' when compared to Israeli aggression (Hage, 2003: 72) betrays intellectual thought for a desire to boost the weaker side. An intellectual commitment to equality translates into an aspiration to symmetrify asymmetric warfare, without adequately considering what the political force one wishes to make equal with one's enemy is actually *for* as well as against. When questioned on the political implications of a decolonisation alliance with Hamas, Pappé (cited in Hussein, 2014: 492) suggests: 'I mean, can we agree, and I think we can, on a set of understandings which leaves some of the questions which are dear to us all – the nature of the state, gender relations, etc. – to leave them open?'

In sum, the priority is to defeat the Zionist monster, which involves an alliance with the Islamist subaltern. All else is of secondary importance.

ONE-STATE NORM, THE ZERO-SUM GAME

Other than Israel, there is no nation state in the world that academic Leftists call for the dismantlement of as a necessity for human progress. 'From the river to the sea, Palestine will be free' is a longstanding chant of pro-Palestinian solidarity activists, which echoes the rallying slogan of Hamas. The academic normalisation of a one-state solution from the river to the sea is a tragedy because it turns the Palestinian-Israeli conflict into a zero-sum game: either the full realisation of a Greater Israel or a return to a historic Palestine, the former of which could feasibly happen and the latter of which would only come about through a major military onslaught and destruction of the nation state of Israel. A global pro-Palestinian movement that calls for one-state ignores the international consensus for a two-state solution and the reality and support inside Israel and occupied Palestine for two-states. Moreover, the external pressure from leftists for one-state, from the river to the sea, serves mostly to benefit the right-wing in Israel and its discourse of one Greater Israel.

One-state advocates are unified in their attack on a 'separatist, essentialist, settler-colonial political Zionism' (Hussein, 2015: 527). However, any academic position that strays from the absolute polarity between settler and native is considered 'assimilationist' or 'worse still, genocidal in effect if not intent' (Busbridge, 2018: 103). Notably, a binational one-state solution, coming from within the body of postcolonial academic literature, is rejected and marginalised as an entrenchment and legitimisation of colonial relations, despite the plea of some to acknowledge the present reality of two national groups and to thus engage with 'the rights claims of Jewish Israelis' to 'alleviate the fears of expulsion in the eventuality of decolonisation, fears also shared by some critical Israelis' (Todorova, 2015: 1381). Anything less than the full unrecognising and undoing of the right of Jewish people to national self-determination is considered immoral and 'an anathema to genuine decolonisation' (Bashir and Busbridge, 2019: 389). Tilley (2015), for example, suggests that seeing a 'Palestinian people' and a 'Jewish people' in need of territorial self-determination is an unacceptable acceptance of an '"ethno-nationalism"' which is '"aberrant, anachronistic and ruinous"' (cited in Bashir and Busbridge, 2019: 397). Busbridge (2018: 101) incisively observes that the absolutist solution of decolonisation is no solution at all since 'a faithful adherence to the paradigm [of settler-colonialism] renders' decolonisation 'largely unachievable, if not impossible': 'thus [the conflict] hurtles from the past to the present into the future, never to be fully extinguished until the native is, or until history itself ends.' This story becomes one of '"either total victory or total failure" (Veracini, 2007)' (Busbridge, 2018: 102), with a victorious one-Palestinian state making room for Jews 'as a neutral and repentant collectivity (Farsakh, 2011: 70)' (Busbridge, 2018: 108).

This zero-sum game can only be understood through its 'Jewish question'. While other nation states have come into existence through settler-colonialism, these are assumed (through the passage of time) fait accomplis. Two reasons are offered as to why Israel must not be considered a fait accompli. The first, Israel arrived too late in a world that has moved on to decolonisation. Here 'the Jewish question' presents as: the Jewish nation state (and the Jews associated with it) are uniquely stuck in the past and are an outstanding impediment to human progress, thus belong to the dustbin of human history. The position of the late historian Tony Judt (2003) reflects this, when he states that 'the problem with Israel [...] is not – as is sometimes suggested – that it is a European "enclave" in the Arab world; but rather that it arrived too late.' The second reason, Zionism is the globalising crucible of colonialism, imperialism, social dispossession, injustice, and repression. Here 'the Jewish question' presents as: Israel and Zionism are the inventories, testers and exporters of global ills. As Veracini (2019: 580) puts it, 'Palestine is today a crucial laboratory of global dispossessions' prior to 'being transferred, that is, *sold* elsewhere'. Further, the western world is 'subliminally' being 'Israelized' (Hage, 2014: 9, cited in Busbridge, 2018: 99) or '"Palestinianized", as Israel exports military techniques and mechanisms of surveillance and social control developed in the occupied territories to the international marketplace' (Collins, 2011, cited in Busbridge, 2018: 98–99). While one aspect of 'the Jewish question' views Zionism as an outlier or latecomer in a postcolonial era, the other aspect sees Zionism as the present-to-future precedent for the ethnic cleansing and genocide of indigenous peoples worldwide: '"expulsions" are the present and the future; Zionism is not a latecomer, it is a precursor' (Veracini, 2019: 580). One-state advocates of the settler-colonialism paradigm thus regard themselves as part of a global decolonisation resistance in 'battle' and 'struggle […] against the processes of Zionism, and against those who collaborate with its processes' (Hussein, 2015: 532). 'Palestine' is hence accorded 'a prophetic role in the global struggle against colonialism and imperialism' (Busbridge, 2018: 98).

CONCLUSION

'The settler colonial paradigm may continue to facilitate transnational solidarity and international sympathy, but may ultimately fail to extend beyond a politics of moral outrage.' (Busbridge, 2018: 111)

'The "othering" of Jews inevitably creates an inequitable economy of compassion and a restrictive arena of solidarity. In its spiritless radicalism it at once turns Israel into the primary source of violence in the world and places Palestinians into a single identity script as victims, only as victims and only as victims of Israel. Just as it subsumes the plurality of Jewish voices to "the Jews" and the plurality of Israeli voices to "Israel", it also subsumes the plurality of Palestinian voices to "the Palestinians" and risks turning them into ciphers of our own resentments.' (Fine and Spencer, 2017: 124)

The postcolonial academic Left approaches the Palestinian-Israeli conflict through a moralistic settler-colonialism lens that sees Israel and Zionism as the ultimate historical vestige and/or harbinger of colonialism, racism and genocide worldwide. This conflict is bound up with a global anti-racist struggle and project of decolonisation in which the priority enemy is Zionist racism. The anti-racist imagination accommodates the Palestinian Islamist suicide bomber as the blowback of racist Zionist oppression: the native punching back above his weight against the Israeli Jewish aggressor. Indeed, in the academic literature presented in this chapter, the degree of separation between the political ideas of Islamism, which has the Jew as evil incarnate, Israel as a cancer to be expunged, and Palestine (and the whole world) in the grip of a global Zionist conspiracy that threatens humanity, is minimal. The settler-colonial paradigm turns Zionism into a monster with an insatiable appetite for ethnic cleansing, who will stop at nothing, up to and including genocide. The Palestinians are made into the victims and only the victims. The moral stains of the twentieth century, the Holocaust and South African apartheid, are brought together to reveal the Israel of the now twenty-first century as the worst of the worst nation states and settler-colonialisms: the Zionist Jews are the contemporary Nazis; the Palestinians are the modern-day victims of the concentration camps. Even when assessed under a seemingly wider comparative lens, to other New World white settler societies, Israel still, incongruently, represents an exceptional harm to humanity which demands undoing as a historical reality. The tragedy of this approach is that it offers no way out for the Palestinians other than a zero-sum game, which itself is a dead end. The leftist imagination here sees Zionism as a particularly deplorable infliction on, and obstacle to, the progress of humanity, and operates zero tolerance for anything other than the dissolution of Israel, along with contrite, shamefaced Jews ready to denounce their collective Jewish identity. This is 'the Jewish question' writ large.

Chapter 4

ESCAPING THE IMPASSE OF THE 'ZIONIST OTHER'

'The Jewish question is *in nuce* a question of antisemitism.' (Fine and Spencer, 2017: 12)

The view that criticism of Israel incites the false accusation of anti-Jewish racism does not hold without an underlying paranoia (conscious or otherwise) that Israel has a phenomenal global power and reach: to single out and perniciously target any critic of Israel anywhere in the world, and dishonestly label them as antisemitic. It is a belief that is based on an imaginary spectre, and it derives from a failure to see Israel as anything other than an essentialised monolithic entity.

While it is the case that a tendency of right-wing defence of Israel weaponises antisemitism in an effort to shut down criticism of the oppressive practices of the Israeli state and military against the Palestinians, it is irrational to regard all defence of Israel as weaponising anti-Jewish racism. Moreover, it is a fantasy to think that Israel (beyond the territories that it has direct control) has unique surreptitious abilities to control world opinion, over and above any other nation state, including big imperialist powers like America, Russia and China. General public opinion across the world, in fact, tends not to favour Israel. Furthermore, while it is true that antisemitism has been weaponised by some of the Zionist Right, it is also true that a significant tendency of left-wing criticism of Israel is based on anti-Jewish racist ideas. Defending criticism of Israel as not racist primarily on the basis that antisemitism has been weaponised in defence of Israel, or consciously holding back from vocalising criticism of Israel for fear of being reproached as racist, is a peculiar and troubling state of affairs. But worse than this, the very idea that subterranean forces are at work to falsely accuse progressive critics of Israel of antisemitism is itself an antisemitic idea. Leftists bemoan this quandary: 'We are not hostile to Jews as Jews, but they label us antisemitic when we criticise Israel's racist occupation of Palestine, and when we then explain that it is racist Israel that malevolently wields antisemitism as a stick to beat us with, we are told that this is antisemitic too!'

By distinguishing between the ruling class, and its oppressive state apparatus, and the general working class population, it is actually straightforward to object to the Israeli state and military occupation of the Palestinian territories without sliding into anti-Jewish racism. With other collectives of people and nation states, the Left is perfectly capable of opposing the ruling class and engaging, agitating and making solidarity with the working class. But not in the case of Israel. The problem here lies in the presence of 'the Jewish question': the idea that something must be done with the harmful Jewish collective. Zionism and Israel are seen to symbolise a particularly objectionable, grave and powerful nationalism, racism, colonialism, and imperialism that must be faced and defeated for the sake of advancing humanity. Jews who are not willing to destroy Israel form part of an exceptionalised and essentialised global Zionism and expansionist Israel, the threatening Other. Laid bare, 'the Jewish question' *is* antisemitism: the world is imagined to be run by Jewish elites, who operate on a supra-national scale, through an invisible reality behind a visible reality, managing the fate of not just Palestinians, but all humankind.

This chapter offers a way out of the impasse created by a Left that designates and dooms Israel, Zionism and the collective body of associated Jews as the epitome of failure, illegitimacy and harm. It follows, these harmful Jews are not members of a universal humanity, unless or until they enlighten themselves to their crimes and seek penance, including doing what no other group of nationally self-defined people has ever done: undo their nation state. This impasse and damnation locks, not releases, the Palestinian-Israeli conflict, because it offers no realistic way forward, while effectively agitating for a war in the name of justice and redress to destroy Israel (since it remains a fantasy that Israeli Jews will willingly give up their national home).

A Marxist tradition exists that is free from 'the Jewish question', that is, free from the 'Enlightenment credo that "we must refuse everything to the Jews as a nation and accord everything to Jews as individuals"', to its contemporary re-emergence in the discourse that values Jews as individuals and devalues Jews as a nation (Fine and Spencer, 2017: 103). In this spirit, this chapter resuscitates the work of the late Professor Maxime Rodinson (1915–2004) on the history of the Palestinian-Israeli conflict. Rodinson was an independent Marxist historian, orientalist and sociologist whose research focused on Islam and the Arab world. His publications include *Islam and Capitalism*; *Muhammad*; *Europe and the Mystique of Islam*; *Israel: A Colonial-Settler State?*; *Cult, Ghetto, and State: The Persistence of the Jewish Question*; *Israel and the Arabs*; *Marxism and the Muslim World*; and *The Arabs*. Rodinson considered the formation of Israel a historical error and a wrong done to the Palestinians, and he pioneered an analysis of Israel as a colonial-settler state. However, Rodinson's work has been either critiqued or ignored by the Left in academia because of his assessment of Zionism in the context of European antisemitism, colonialism and nationalism – that is, beyond the framework of a colonial model of racism and 'the Jewish question' – and his acceptance of the reality of Israel as a nation state on pre-1967 borders (see: Nir and Wainwright, 2018; Wolfe, 2012).

Rodinson's legacy has been more generally displaced, as I explained in Chapter Three, by the fashionable intellectual trend which positions Zionism and Israel firmly into an enemy camp of racism-and-colonialism-incarnate. The Palestinian-Israeli conflict, for Rodinson, is not an exceptional tragedy produced by the Jews, despite the legitimate grievances of the Palestinians, and its resolution is not one that exceptionally demands the erasure of Israel. I revisit, also, the writings of Karl Marx, Vladmir Lenin and Leon Trotsky on 'the Jewish question', in order to demonstrate a classical Marxist approach to political and human emancipation which is actually *free from* and *not tied to* 'the Jewish question' – an approach that is alive in Rodinson's work. Marx, Lenin and Trotsky offer a crucial Marxist steer to genuine universalism and consistent democracy on the national question which remains relevant today as a route forward for the Left that is obsessed and weighed down by its 'Zionist Other'.

RODINSON ON THE COLONIAL ORIGINS OF ISRAEL

'Once again in the course of human history, events in a tiny Middle Eastern province [...] have shaken the world and unleashed fierce passions from San Francisco to Karachi. The province is that little patch of Palestinian soil, barren and inhospitable, in which only the imagination of half-starved nomads could see "a land flowing with milk and honey".' (Rodinson, 1968: 7)

Setting a destiny for the conflict between Israel and Palestine was the concurrent development from the late nineteenth century onwards of Jewish national aspiration for territory known as Palestine and Arab national aspiration for the same territory. Palestinian-Arab nationalism emerged both as a consequence of British and French colonial expansion into the Ottoman Empire – which imported the idea of the nation state that, in turn, permeated all major Arab political ideologies at the time – and as a response to early discrete Jewish settlement in Palestine (then an Arab province of the Ottoman Empire and commonly regarded as a southern region of Syria) (Rodinson, 1968).

Rodinson (1973, 1983) points out that the Jews most drawn to the early Zionist promise of a Jewish homeland, and who gave this nationalist movement its strength, were the persecuted poor of Eastern Europe and Czarist Russia. These Jewish masses were not colonialist or imperialist in their motives, rather, they 'were essentially moved by deep disgust with the oppressive conditions they had been subjected to' (Rodinson, 1973: 35). The colonial character of Zionism came from 'one small detail that seemed to be of no importance: Palestine was inhabited by another people' (ibid: 36). The fact that Palestine was occupied by an original population was ignored and, when this fact did become more widely known, it was met with general indifference. This, Rodinson (1973: 37–38) explains, was:

> 'an indifference linked to European supremacy, which [...] planted in the minds of even the most deprived of those who shared in it the idea that any territory outside Europe was open to European occupation. From this point of view the Zionist brand of utopia was essentially no different from socialist utopias like Cabet's Icaria. It was a matter of finding an empty territory – empty not necessarily in the sense of actual absence of inhabitants, but rather of a kind of cultural barrenness.'

The approach taken by Theodor Herzl and the Zionist Organisation was consistent with the European colonial expansionism of the nineteenth and twentieth centuries. Rodinson (1973: 40–41) states, there is 'no reason whatsoever to be surprised or even indignant at this':

> 'Except for a section (only a section) of the European socialist parties and a few rare revolutionary and liberal elements, colonialization at the time was essentially taken to mean the spreading of progress, civilization and well-being. The world at that time was dominated by the great European imperialist powers. Any

undertaking aiming to bring about a political transformation would have to obtain at least their consent and, better yet, their support. For this, it would have to offer advantages for these powers and fit into their plans. And that was a consideration that any realistic mind would have to take into account. Around the same period, the father of Moslem nationalism, Jamal ad-din al-Afghani, was spending his life, like Herzl, sounding out which powers might back his plans, attempting to play off one against the other.'

On the courting of European imperialist powers, the King of Greater Syria and then Iraq, Emir Faisal, sought the protection of Great Britain in a plan to exchange Palestine to the Jews for a large independent Arab state that a future Jewish state would provide with technical aid – an ambition that he dropped amid the reality that the Arab masses would be against it (Rodinson, 1973). In brief, the prevailing colonial philosophy in Europe explains and is responsible for the fact that the actual population of Palestine was generally ignored by the early Zionists. This does not excuse this fact, rather it explains it as one that was not exceptional. The class composition and motivations of the early Zionist movement were more nuanced than an equation of Zionism with racist and capitalist conquest infers. Antisemitism in Eastern Europe and Russia was a key factor in driving poor and persecuted people towards the escape route promised by the Zionist leaders. The seed for future conflict lay in the absence of consideration by those in the Zionist movement to those who already had Palestine as their home. These Jews were not innately and markedly racist. It was the European zeitgeist at this time which was ideologically racist in regarding territory beyond Europe as in need of progress and civilisation. Finally, it was not just the Zionist leadership in pursuit of a partnership with a European imperialist power, other Arab nationalist leaders sought this also as the means to fulfil their projects.

The First World War marked a new era for the Middle East, with the Ottoman Empire siding with Germany and Austria-Hungary against Britain, France and Russia, and the ruling classes of the latter three drawing up the secret 1916 Sykes-Picot Agreement: a plan, in the event of victory, to carve up control of the Ottoman Empire (Rodinson, 1968). While the British promised Arab independence in exchange for their cooperation during this war, on 2 November 1917, the British pledged, in the Balfour Declaration, a Jewish national homeland in Palestine (which would serve its colonial interests as a base to protect the Suez Canal and the route between Egypt and India, and to counter French influence in the region) (Rodinson, 1968, 1973). Coming five days after the Bolshevik-led Russian Revolution, an additional aim of the Declaration was to support the Russian counter-revolutionary Kerensky (Rodinson, 1973). The League of Nations officially granted British Mandate over Palestine on 24 July 1922, thus ratifying the Balfour Declaration. The significance of the Balfour Declaration cannot be understated since it helped realise the Zionist ambition. Together with the Arab âm an-nakba of 1920 (the year when France announced control of Syria and Lebanon, and Britain of Iraq and Palestine), it explains a deep and enduring Arab resentment against European colonial powers of which Jewish immigration to Palestine was seen as part of (Rodinson, 1968, 1973). In other words, while some Arab nationalist leaders sought British imperialist protection, none were given what the Jewish nationalist project of Zionism was given. From the perspective of the Arab world, it is understandable then that Zionism was seen and opposed as European colonialism.

From 1924 to 1931, it is estimated that 29 out of every 100 Jews immigrating to Palestine left after a short stay, with, in 1927, more departures than arrivals; during this period, a majority of Jews in Palestine considered a purely Jewish state unrealistic (Rodinson, 1968). The definitive turning point to the actualisation of a Jewish nation state was Nazi Germany's persecution of Jews in Europe: 'anti-Semitism played a capital role in gathering together an entire group that was otherwise on the road to disintegration. Zionism played no significant role [...] before 1939' (Rodinson, 1983: 164).

Regardless of the fact that Zionism had the sealed promise of the Balfour Declaration, it would not have translated into the reality of a nation state, if it were not for the fact that a critical mass of Jews were fleeing for their lives from the horror of Nazi antisemitism and were denied emigration elsewhere in the western world. Along with European fascism and the 1936–39 Arab revolt in Palestine (primarily in protest against Jewish immigration), the base of Zionist support was further fuelled by anger against the responses of the British to managing Arab hostility: the 1937 Peel Commission partition plan and 1939 White Paper calling for a limit to Jewish immigration and land purchase, and a binational state under British control for ten years, in which Jews would be kept to one third of the population (Rodinson, 1968, 1973). By the end of 1943, there was a critical number of Jews in Palestine willing to push for a Jewish state in opposition to the British.

This changing dynamic between the Zionist movement and the British imperialist power did not alter the fact that 'Great Britain was the motor force [...] by force of arms' that 'conquered the territory to be occupied', it simply explains that Britain 'met with the anger of its "colonists" when it thought it could limit their progress toward completely controlling the said territory' (Rodinson, 1973: 84). A revitalised Zionism was expressed in the 1942 Biltmore Program, proposed by David Ben Gurion, calling for: the establishment of a Jewish nation state in all of Palestine, the creation of a Jewish army, the rejection of the 1939 White Paper, and unlimited immigration under the control of the Jewish Agency (Rodinson, 1973). While a decade previously, a large minority of the *Yishuv* seriously considered the call for a binational state, this moment had now passed. A glorified 'struggle against "British tyranny"' commenced alongside the exigent task of saving Jewish survivors of the Holocaust; in all, 'the Arab problem' was pushed 'into the background, where it was almost forgotten' (Rodinson, 1973: 64). With Britain's decision in February 1947 to withdraw from Palestine, the Arab leaders' rejection of the United Nations partition plan announced in November 1947, and David Ben Gurion's declaration of the nation state of Israel on 14 May 1948, the withdrawal of British troops from Palestine on 15 May 1948 'made the bloody confrontation inevitable':

'In this three-tiered struggle, once the battle against the mother-country oppressor was ended, the battle against the oppressed-in-the-making could begin. To be sure, the colonial situation could have been left behind at this point and two states, recognized by the UN, could have entered into the realm of international politics.' (Rodinson, 1973: 66)

However, Rodinson (1973: 66) stresses, for 'the Arab masses, acceptance of the UN decisions would have meant unconditional capitulation to a European *diktat*'.

In sum, a new population of Europeans settled on an already occupied territory whose people refused such a settlement and these settlers 'came from that world which was everywhere known as the world of the colonizers' (Rodinson, 1968: 215); the critical momentum for this mass settlement was murderous antisemitism. The colonial origins of Israel stem from the facts that Palestine had an original population that was ignored by the Zionist movement and that the Zionist plan to establish a Jewish state in Palestine was ratified through the British Balfour Declaration. The Arabs, Rodinson (1973: 53) remarks, were 'most justified' in seeing 'the transplanting of a new and foreign element' of mostly Europeans onto Palestinian territory as an imposition 'by a European power'. The specific colonial relations have been 'less relations of exploitation than of domination', with the Zionist determination to rule over territory rather than another people (ibid: 86). 'Wanting to create a purely Jewish, or predominantly Jewish, state' in Palestine has inevitably led to 'a colonial-type situation' – with 'the development (completely normal, sociologically speaking) of a racist state of mind' – and to a violent confrontation between two self-defined national groups of people (Rodinson, 1973: 74). Significantly, Rodinson (1973: 105) adds, in an endnote, 'only a racist or mystical concept of "Jewishness"' could explain the 'shock' of others that the 'conditions' which 'everywhere else bring about a state with a racist mentality (an ethnic cleavage coinciding with a social change) are also at work in the case of Jews.' In other words, only a racist approach that signifies Jews as harmful to humanity would express outrage that a Jewish nation state is racist, when, in fact, the formation of nation states as ethnic splits are generally racist. The colonial and racist dimension of the Jewish nation state is here elucidated as both general and specific, but as not exceptional.

RODINSON ON RESOLUTION TO THE PALESTINIAN-ISRAELI CONFLICT

The conclusions that Rodinson (1968, 1973, 1983) draws from his assessment of Israel as a colonial-settler state are radically different from the damnation cast by, and the impasse implied from, the postcolonial paradigm of settler-colonialism explored in Chapter Three. Notably, his case for a 'two nations, two states' resolution. Rodinson (1968) understands Zionism as a manifestation of nationalism that pursued its project in an era of decolonisation; moreover, he recognises that, for many in the Arab world, Zionism is synonymous with imperialism, colonialism and capitalism, and is bound up with the Palestinian refugees as the living symbol of injustice. Indeed, Rodinson (1968: 232) observes, a 'case could be made out for giving the Arab cause a near-absolute value', since, after all, a section of the Left internationally 'maintains that Israel is a bastion of imperialism' and 'her very existence' is 'a threat to progress and liberty in the world at large, and in the Arab world in particular'. Such notions, however, are reminiscent of 'the most vulgar ideological Marxism of the Stalin era' (Rodinson, 1968: 233). Declining such abstract postulates, Rodinson (1968: 234) states that: 'Israel, with all the limitations which her dependence entails, has a will and a purpose of her own. She does not automatically obey all the injunctions of the United States, nor yet those of that indefinable monster which this over-schematized Marxism calls "imperialism".'

Israel is, instead, 'primarily interested in survival', which a current of Israeli politics (he writes in 1968) advocates through 'expansion' (Rodinson, 1968: 234). Rodinson (1973: 87) further discerns that while Israel could apply its technical superiority for economic dominance of other economies, its ability to do so is 'greatly diminished by the smallness of its territory, its difficulties with its nearest neighbors, and perhaps especially its own economic dependence on the European-American powers'. As such, he argues, Israel is an ally of imperialist powers through a 'political choice' that was largely 'imposed by the circumstances surrounding the formation and birth of the state' (ibid: 87). In other words, Israel is not an exceptionally harmful colonialist and imperialist power. For Rodinson (1973: 92), awareness of the 'colonial character' of Israel helps expound 'why the pressure of [...] events does so much to thrust Israel into the camp of the Western powers', the responses of the Arab people, and how an alternative course for Israel requires (and necessitates) 'heroic efforts on the part of progressive elements in Israel'. Committed to challenging 'both the intemperate idealization of the [Zionist] movement by Zionists' and 'the no less frenzied "diabolization"' of this movement by anti-Zionists, Rodinson (1983: 150–151) provides an objective critique of Zionism as a nationalist phenomenon seeking imperialist support:

'Criticism of the methods of Zionism is inoperative and insufficient in itself. [...] Divided into many divergent branches, the Zionist movement has the normal characteristics of any ideological movement of this type. [...] The Zionist organizations have employed the usual methods, certain groups and individuals seeking to attain their ends with more scruples than others. Cases of both self-sacrifice and personal exploitation of the ideology can be found, as well as instances of brutality and humanity, examples of totalitarianism based entirely on efficacy and others in which human factors have been taken into account. Naturally, any universalist critique of nationalism in general also targets Zionism, for in it we find all the unpleasant features of nationalism, beginning with contempt for the rights of others, in a manner declared and cynical by some and masked by others, often transfigured by ideology and thus rendered unconscious among many, disguised in their own eyes by secondary moral justifications.'

If it is deemed that Rodinson fails to go far enough in his critique, then it is because there exists a leftist worldview, in contrast to Rodinson's, that is bound to 'the Jewish question', which – rather than applying a universalist critique of nationalism, racism and colonialism – is fixated with the idea of an exceptionally and essentially bad collective of Jews.

'What are the consequences to be drawn from' the 'diagnosis' of Israel as a colonial-settler state, Rodinson (1973: 90–91) asks:

'Preach holy war against the intruders and demand that they be forcibly evicted and cast into the sea in the name of a universal conscience that was very slow to condemn colonialism? Brand them as criminals in the eyes of the whole world? Demand that, barefoot and with a rope already around their neck, they come pleading for forgiveness for their original sin? [...] It is up to the

Arabs, who are the ones who have been wronged, to determine what their policy toward Israel will be. The role of others does not seem to me to be to urge them to seek military solutions. […] Colonists and colonizers are not monsters with human faces whose behavior defies rational explanation, as one might think from reading left-wing intellectuals. I am anti-colonialist and anti-racist, but I cannot on that account give up attempting to explain colonialism and racism in terms of the most widespread and commonplace social and psychological factors, which no one should claim lie beyond reach. Belonging to a colonising group is not the unspeakable and unpardonable crime it is thought to be in cafes along Saint-Germain and Saint-Michel boulevards. Who is innocent of this charge? The only variable lies in the time that has elapsed since the usurping was done. The human conscience sooner or later accepts the idea that long-time use establishes a valid claim. History is full of faits accomplis.'

A current of the contemporary academic Left echoes the sanctimony of the left-wing intellectuals which Rodinson refers to, by moralistically singling out and demonising Zionism and Israel of the crimes of colonialism and racism that others too are guilty of, and effectively demanding the military-based dissolution of Israel. 'Colonists and colonizers are not monsters', Rodinson (1973: 91) reminds us, and yet Zionism, Israel and the related Jewish collective have been made into a monster: a leviathan representing the ills and threats of the racist capitalist world. As if in retort to much of the present-day academic Left, Rodinson (1983: 156) remarks, 'I have sometimes been told that to acknowledge the colonial nature of Israel is to imply the necessity of de-colonization in accordance with the logic of the liberation movements of people today.' However, he continues, the ending of a colonial situation has several possible meanings:

'In general, the colonial situation ends when all relations of domination, oppression, and exploitation end. In the case of settler-colonialism, this does not require that the new inhabitants be expelled and return to their place of origin. Nor that they in turn be placed under the domination of the original inhabitants. […] Indeed, the oppressor is not an oppressor absolutely and for all time. People are drawn by circumstances or ideologies to engage in the practice of oppression, and all the peoples of the world have gone through stages in which they have inflicted oppression on others and have suffered it themselves in turn.' (Rodinson, 1983: 156–157)

Against the tendency to single out Israel as having an exceptional colonial essence, Rodinson (1968, 1973) engages in a genuinely comparative assessment. Since Cromwell, he explains, the British colonial power occupied Catholic Ireland and colonised the Protestant-majority Ulster, where the minority Catholic population was discriminated against. While the Irish swore 'never to recognize this amputation of their homeland', and there is no doubt that this forceful amputation was 'unjust', one day in February 1965, the existence of Ulster was recognised (Rodinson, 1973: 92). Rodinson (1973: 92) continues:

'The Jews of Israel too are people like other people. Some of them have hammered out an illusory ideology to which they have sacrificed themselves as well as a great deal of effort and many human lives. They are not alone. Many are those who have suffered much but have looked with indifference upon the sufferings and rights of others. Many went there because it was the life preserver thrown to them. They most assuredly did not first engage in scholarly research to find out if they had a right to it according to Kantian morality or existentialist ethics. It is accordingly useless to reproach them for it.'

'As for the right of the Israelis to continue to exist as a national community on the land they acquired in this way', Rodinson (1973: 87–88) advances, 'one can only claim to have left the colonial process behind when the native group, as a result of negotiated concessions, comes to accept this autonomy.' He continues, the colonial origins of the Pied-Noirs in Algeria (i.e., the population of French and European descent) did not stop the Algerian National Liberation Front from recognising their rights. Indeed, the departure of the Pied-Noirs was not a consequence of expulsion but of their refusal to adapt to the new situation of an independent Algeria. Likewise, there is no demand to drive the white-identifying population out of South Africa because of their colonial origins, rather, they are expected to coexist with the black-identifying population as equals. Tackling the question of justice and redress, Rodinson (1968: 231–232) reasons:

> 'If the consequences of pressing a just claim are liable to be calamitous and unjust, and too fraught with practical difficulties, there may be grounds for suggesting that it be renounced. The wrong done to the Arabs by the Israelis is very real. However, it is only too common throughout history. Innumerable violations of rights of this nature have taken place since the beginnings of human society. Sometimes one side, sometimes the other has been the ultimate beneficiary. […] We may therefore plead with the Arabs to accept the *fait accompli*.'

However, Rodinson (1983: 15) cautions, Arab acceptance of this fait accompli will not be the outcome of Zionists telling them 'how right it was, by virtue of admirable "Jewish values" or "inalienable" rights dating back to Solomon, to attack them, drive them out, and take their lands', it would be far wiser to acknowledge the wrong which was done and offer meaningful compensation.

In Rodinson's history of the Palestinian-Israeli conflict, there is no presence of 'the Jewish question', that is, the idea that one must address the exceptional harm done by the Jewish collective to humanity, and, as such, there is no exceptionalisation of Israel as a colonial-settler state. While deploring 'the historical error of the creation of the state of Israel on Arab land', Rodinson (1983: 14–15) recognises the existence of a new national group, that can neither be considered a religious community which can be accommodated into an Arabic nation, nor be regarded 'a heterogenous collection of gangs of occupiers who could be sent back where they came from'. 'For at least a protracted historical period', he states, 'one can speak only in terms of the coexistence of two states' (Rodinson, 1983: 225). Two national and ethnic groups exist and if one is to avoid 'the danger of the domination of one by the other', both self-defined national entities must have the right to political representation in defence of their interests and hopes (ibid: 160). A 'two nations, two states' resolution that recognises the nation state of Israel proper, extinguishes Israel's relations of domination, exploitation and oppression in the Occupied Palestinian Territories, enacts the Palestinians' right to a fully independent nation state on the land occupied by Israel from 1967, and provides compensation for the Palestinian refugees from the 1948–49 war, is the direction that, after a period of peace, might lead to more progressive co-existence between Jews and Arabs.

RODINSON ON ZIONISM, ANTI-ZIONISM AND ANTISEMITISM

An understanding of Zionism as an especially deplorable colonialism, imperialism, nationalism and racism is commonplace on the academic and activist Left, as is the outright rejection of anti-Zionism as antisemitism. Rodinson (1983: 138) provides a useful interlocution here:

'For some, Zionism is the product of a permanent national aspiration on the part of all Jews, and for that very reason legitimate and benevolent. For others, it represents an essential betrayal of universalist values, whether those of the Jewish religion, liberal humanism, or proletarian internationalism. For yet others (and sometimes for the same people), it is above all a malevolent product either of the noxious essence of the Jews or of imperialist capitalism.'

The idea of Zionism as an exceptional affront to universal human values and as an innate entity of Jewish imperialist capitalism is an expression of the Left's 'Jewish question'. Far from overcoming the question of what is to be done with the harmful Jewish Other, far too many have 'the Jewish question' central to their anti-colonialist, anti-imperialist, anti-racist and anti-capitalist politics. On anti-Zionism, Rodinson (1983: 148) is critical of the failure of those using the term Zionism to differentiate between Israeli nationalism or patriotism, pro-Israeli opinion, recognition of the legitimacy of the nation state of Israel on pre-1967 borders, observation that the nation state of Israel was formed, and the Palestine-centric standpoint of religious Jews; instead, all of these ideological currents are crudely 'thrown together in the concept of "Zionism"'. Furthermore, he questions the more polemical position that characterises as Zionism, 'any defence of the individual rights of Jews, any sympathy for the Jews, or any criticism of the Arab position' (ibid: 148). Writing off people with a Zionist slur is both politically inaccurate and foolish, because:

'Some of these people who support the existence of Israel do not hesitate, in other circumstances, to condemn the practices of the Israeli government and even to back certain Palestinian demands. [...] [One] cannot simply write off people who, at a given moment, have expressed sentiments of sympathy towards

> Israel and the Israeli people [...] [One] must not believe that such people are radically incapable of understanding the situation of the Arabs and Palestinians.' (Rodinson, 1983: 166–167)

Contrariwise, Rodinson (1983: 183) maintains that the 'exasperation' felt by anti-Zionists at the weaponisation of antisemitism and 'the mythification' of 'Judeophobias' by some Zionists is 'psychologically understandable'. However, to then 'deny or minimize the wrongs suffered by the Jews' as a response 'is no less stupid for being understandable' (ibid: 183). While it is true that the Zionist movement sought and gained the support of British and later American imperialist powers, Zionism 'cannot be considered simply the product of a particular class of Jews': 'The tragedy of the situation of the Jews in Europe after 1934, and especially after 1939, on the contrary won it the support of many Jews of all social layers and all ideological tendencies who had long remained reticent' (Rodinson, 1983: 145).

For even the Jews that had assimilated and 'drifted away', 'anti-Semitism acted to re-awaken Jewish identity' – a 'position [...] comprehensible from a human point of view' (Rodinson, 1983: 164). There is a crucial difference here in how the intersection of Zionism and antisemitism is understood. For a dominant tendency in the postcolonial application of the settler-colonialism paradigm, Zionism as racism is a *continuum* of antisemitism; in contrast, for Rodinson (1983), antisemitism *fuelled* Zionism: the Holocaust was the historical turning point in the fate of Zionism. In branding Zionism as racism and framing the victims of antisemitism as translating and weaponising their victimhood into the racist repression of Palestinians, the fact which is banished is that without the murderous escalation of antisemitism in Europe, there would not have been the critical mass of refugees that made Israel a reality on Palestinian land. This degradation of the Holocaust both misrecognises Jewish identity and distorts the course of human history that led to 1948: the moment when the right of Jewish national self-determination was realised and the right of Palestinian national self-determination on the same territory was displaced. The fact that a grave injustice was done to the Palestinians, and continues to be done, does not negate the significance of the Holocaust to Jewish identity.

The postcolonial positioning of Palestinian Islamist resistance (including the suicide bombings of the Second Intifada) as part of the decolonisation and anti-racism struggle effectively evades the question of how this resistance advances an anti-Zionism that bleeds into antisemitism. Rodinson (1983: 187) observes that the racialisation made by Islamist organisations of Zionism with 'the supposed general pernicious character of the Jews and Judaism' – which has gained popularity in the Muslim world – is a serious impediment to the Palestinian plight:

> 'Zionist propaganda does its work by arguing that all the anti-Zionist efforts of the Arabs and others are motivated by anti-Semitic propensities, by hatred of the Jews in general. [...] The Arabs and some of their friends ought to understand that they are in effect aiding Zionist and Arabophobic propaganda whenever they denounce a Zionist act or thesis while explaining it, or appearing to explain it, by the eternal maleficence of the Jewish people, while accordingly seeking analogies for it in Jewish history, or while suggesting that the persecution of the Jews was deserved, or did not actually take place, or was minimal.'

The consequence of Islamist antisemitism and its popularisation in the Muslim world is to drive Jews further into the arms of Zionism. After all, Rodinson (1983: 189) states: 'How can any Jew – in any of the many senses of the term – remain indifferent to Arab assertions claiming that all Jews are maleficent, and how could such assertions fail to incline them to lend a more favourable ear to Zionist theses?'

A politics committed to the Palestinian plight and yet bound to 'the Jewish question' and anti-Jewish racism cannot deliver a resolution to the conflict, rather, such a politics steers the conflict in a direction that entrenches the right-wing in Israel and aids its expansionist project.

RODINSON'S LEGACY FOR DECOLONISING THE UNIVERSITY

Decolonisation of the university is a contemporary intellectual and political project that extends from postcolonial academic work. It aims for university curricula to critically assess and challenge 'white', Eurocentric, Western and global North knowledge systems that are structured by the power relations of colonialism. As such, 'decolonise the university' is a particular anti-racist demand (which views racism through a colonial model) in the context of higher education research and teaching. Eve Tuck and K. Wayne Yang (2012), in their seminal paper, 'Decolonization is not a metaphor', issue a warning against depoliticising the decolonisation of the university project, urging that the political goal of returning dispossessed indigenous land and ending settler-colonialism remains central. Specifically, they argue that the settler must not relinquish the burden of the crimes committed by their ancestors against native people and that there is no option of reconciliation, since this implies a commonality between settler and native that does not and cannot exist. They thus call out settler '*moves to innocence*' as 'problematically' attempting 'to reconcile settler guilt and complicity, and rescue settler futurity' (Tuck and Yang, 2012: 3). Tuck and Yang (2012: 35) similarly insist on 'an ethic of incommensurability, which guides moves that unsettle innocence [...] in contrast to aims of reconciliation, which motivate settler moves to innocence.'

This thinking is reflected in the postcolonial settler-colonialism paradigm applied to the Palestinian-Israeli conflict: two national groups are *deliberately* judged by different standards; accordingly, Palestinians have a right to national self-determination while Israeli Jews have no such right. As I will go on to demonstrate, through the work of Lenin and Trotsky, this ethic of incommensurability cuts against the basic democratic right of all self-defined groups of people to national self-determination, and (with this right realised) the hope of future union. Denying commonality fuels the impasse that locks in a stand-off between two opposing and co-created politicised identities of 'settler' and 'native' by locking in settler-*as*-'settler' and native-*as*-'native', which then shuts down the possibility of people coming together.

In her book *States of Injury*, the political scientist Wendy Brown (1995: 5) defends the socialist vision of democracy that, one day, 'humans might govern themselves by governing together'. Applying the distinction that Marx (1843) makes in *On the Jewish Question* between political emancipation and human emancipation, she critiques the abandonment of the goal of freedom (human emancipation) in progressive political thought and activism, specifically, trends within philosophy and feminist, postcolonial and cultural theory that have foreclosed on socialism. Brown (1995: 61) asks: 'To what extent do identity politics require a standard internal to existing society against which to pitch their claims, a standard that not only preserves capitalism from critique, but sustains the invisibility and inarticulateness of class – not accidentally, but endemically?'

In the settler-versus-native dichotomy, the native requires the settler as *its Other*, as the 'standard internal to existing society against which to pitch their claims' (ibid: 61), and thus the prospect of class alliance between settler and native disappears. Furthermore, drawing on Nietzsche, Brown (1995: 68) explains how politicised identities generate *ressentiment* and, as such, lead to a dead end rather than a pathway to togetherness and freedom: '*Ressentiment* in this context is a triple achievement: it produces an affect (rage, righteousness) that overwhelms the hurt; it produces a culprit responsible for the hurt; and it produces a site of revenge to displace the hurt (a place to inflict hurt as the sufferer has been hurt).'

What we have, she concludes, is a contemporary political condition that gives history 'weight but no trajectory, mass but no coherence', and 'force but no direction' (Brown, 1995: 71). The journey back to the dream of freedom requires superseding the politics of '"I am"' – which fixes identity into a moral hierarchy and breeds *ressentiment*, impedes connection and circumvents freedom – with a politics of '"I want this for us"' (ibid: 75).

The deadlock of academic Left analysis on the Palestinian-Israeli conflict derives from a damnation of the Jewish, Israeli and Zionist 'settler' and an idealisation of the Palestinian 'native'. The feat of *ressentiment* in this context is the catharsis of rage and self-righteousness against the enemy body of Jews represented by Israel and Zionism, which is expressed through various sites of protest that proclaim revenge in the name of pro-Palestinian solidarity. For much of the Left, it is as if the Palestinian-Israeli conflict is *the* siphon for all *ressentiments*. It is as if, for the Left that has the luxury of residing from afar, this 'war without ends or end' (Brown, 1995: 71) is needed to sustain the Self's political identity. Rodinson's legacy for the contemporary decolonisation agenda is a lost one, because (in the spirit of reconciliation) he reminds us that: 'No people is saintly. No people is intrinsically good or bad eternally and by their essence. No people is destined always to be victims. All peoples have been victims and executioners by turns, and all peoples count among their number both victims and executioners' (Rodinson, 1983: 182).

Nevertheless, Rodinson's work has the potential of reorientating the decolonise the university project in a direction that has the hope of humans governing themselves by governing together.

MARX'S *ON THE JEWISH QUESTION*

For a body of scholarship, all three figures of classical Marxism – Marx, Lenin and Trotsky – are considered the founders of a Marxist tradition hostile to a Jewish collectivity (see, for example: Cesarani, 2004; Cohen, 2005; Cohen, 2004; Rapoport, 1990; Vaksberg, 1994; Wistrich, 1979). Cohen (2005) asserts that while Marx was 'a classic case of the self-hating Jew' (61), Lenin's contribution to the Jewish question, although not per se antisemitic, was 'a capitulation to anti-semitism' (72). On Trotsky, Wistrich (1979) proclaims that, like Marx, he displayed a 'peculiar neurosis' in that 'anything self-consciously "Jewish" was intolerable' (11), including the 'complete rejection of the very principle of Jewish national self-determination' (2). Some of this scholarship dates Marxist hostility to the Jews from Marx's *On the Jewish Question*, where, it is claimed, Marx displayed 'particular venom for the Jews' and 'inadvertently encouraged the anti-Semitic myth that Jews controlled the world's money markets' (Rapoport, 1990: 9; see also, Wistrich, 1979; Cohen, 1984). Others date Marxist hostility from the late 1890s, specifically, with the opposition of Lenin and Trotsky to the demand for national cultural autonomy by the secular Jewish socialist party, the Bund (see: Golan, 2001).

By examining the original writings of Marx, Lenin and Trotsky on 'the Jewish question', commencing with Marx, I show that all three founders of classical Marxism address 'the Jewish question' by arguing for an emancipatory politics *free from* 'the Jewish question'. The purpose of excavating their contributions is not simply to challenge the claim that classical Marxism is hostile to Jews, it is to remind the Left of a Marxist tradition for political and human emancipation which is genuinely universal and that on the national question recognises the centrality of consistent democracy: that is, the *unconditional* democratic right of *all* self-defined groups of people to national self-determination. This universalism and consistent democracy is reflected in Rodinson's work on the Palestinian-Israeli conflict.

Fine and Spencer (2017) disagree with both the derogatory view that Marx was antisemitic and the apologetic view that translates Marx's language regarding Jewish people into the language of anti-capitalism. The legacy of these two views, they note, is either the dismissal of Marxism as antisemitism or a leftist approach to 'the Jewish question' that treats this question as real rather than as a reactionary racist idea. The problem with the view that Marx was antisemitic, Fine and Spencer (2017) point out, is that aside from the second of the two-part essay, *On the Jewish Question* (which is part of a debate with the left Hegelian Bruno Bauer), there is no evidence of anti-Jewish sentiment in Marx's writings. On the contrary, as McLellan (1980) observes, in the passages of the *Holy Family* that deal with the debate with Bauer on 'the Jewish question', Marx makes it plain that he assesses the political maturity of a state by the extent to which its Jewish population are emancipated within it, and that he regards it nonsensical for civil society to deny Jewish people their equal rights. In this section, I argue that Marx responds to 'the Jewish question' that occupies Bauer, by arguing for political and human emancipation without specific demands placed on 'Jews as Jews'.

In *On the Jewish Question*, Marx (1843, in McLellan, 1977: 41) explains that, for Bauer, the universal significance of the Jewish question lies in 'the relationship of religion to the state, of the opposition between religious prejudice and political emancipation', such that the Jewish question will only be solved when the Jews stop obeying their own religious laws and choose to participate fully in state life. As such, Bauer is bound to 'the Jewish question' by placing the demand on Jewish people to give up their religion to gain access to political rights. Marx (1845) later remarks in the *Holy Family* of Bauer's book, *The Jewish Question* (1843), 'the criticism of political emancipation changes into a criticism of the Jewish religion.' Marx

(1843, in McLellan, 1977: 42–43) challenges Bauer's error, both in failing to consider what kind of emancipation is in question and in demanding of the Jews the relinquishment of their religion:

> 'Bauer asks the Jews: Does your standpoint give you the right to seek political emancipation? But we ask the reverse question: Has the standpoint of political emancipation the right to require from the Jews the abolition of Judaism and from all men [*sic*] the abolition of religion?'

Marx (1843, in McLellan, 1977) acknowledges the 'great [...] real, practical' progress of political emancipation (47), but on its limits he argues that while the capitalist state abolishes in its own way the distinctions of class, birth, profession and education, by declaring them 'to be unpolitical differences', it allows them 'to have an effect in their own manner' (45). Hence humankind leads a twofold existence: 'a heavenly one' as (ideally) communal beings in a political community, and 'an earthy one' as (materially) private, alienated, egoistic individuals in civil society (ibid: 46). For Marx, North America presents the capitalist perfection of the political state (as a constitutional and secular one), so it is the most illuminating example to explore the relationship of religion to the state. In North America, he concludes, Bauer's Jewish question is a secular one, with, in actual fact, not the disappearance but the flourishment of religion, which tells us (in contrast to Bauer's claim) that 'the existence of religion does not contradict or impede the perfection of the state' (Marx, 1843, in McLellan, 1977: 43).

What is inherent in political emancipation, Marx (1843) spells out, is a gap between human beings as, ideally, public members of a universal state (or 'citizens') and, materially, private, egoistic members of civil society (or 'bourgeois'). Private rights are clarified thus as the right to property, the right to religion, and so on, which are innately 'bourgeois' and the basis of the separation of human beings from one another. The shift of religion from political state to civil society (from public law to private right) accordingly expresses the exile of communal existence. In contradistinction to Bauer, who cannot see beyond political emancipation and 'the Jewish question', for Marx (1843, in McLellan, 1977: 44): 'The question of the relationship of political emancipation to religion becomes for us a question of the relationship of political emancipation to human emancipation.'

In the second part of *On the Jewish Question*, Marx explicitly turns Bauer's theological question into a material one: as Marx (1843, in McLellan, 1977: 58) puts it, what is of relevance is 'not the Sabbath Jew', but 'the actual secular Jew'. To expose religion as a spiritual concealment of an egoistic, material existence, Marx insists on asking 'what particular social element needs to be overcome in order to abolish Judaism?' (ibid: 58). He proceeds:

'Money is the jealous god of Israel before whom no other god may stand. Money debases all the gods of man [*sic*] and turns them into commodities. Money is the universal, self-constituted value of all things. It has therefore robbed the whole world, human as well as natural, of its own values. Money is the alienated essence of man's work and being, this alien essence dominates him and he adores it.' (Marx, 1843, in McLellan, 1977: 60)

To repeat, money debases *not only* 'the jealous god of Israel' but 'all the gods of man [*sic*]' (ibid: 60). Here Marx (1843, in McLellan, 1977: 56) is polemically reinforcing his earlier point on political emancipation, that: 'Man [*sic*] was [...] not freed from religion; he received freedom of religion. He was not freed from property; he received freedom of property. He was not freed from the egoism of trade; he received freedom to trade.'

The contempt Marx exhibits is not for the Jew but for the debasement of theory, art, history, nature and human relations by religion, property, commodities and commerce. In this vein, he goes on to deplore the bartering of women, 'the species-relationship itself', as 'an object of commerce!' (Marx, 1843, in McLellan, 1977: 60). He concludes his debate with Bauer – who argues that the political emancipation of the Jews is contingent on the Jews giving up their religion – by stating, 'the social emancipation of the Jew implies the emancipation of society from Judaism' (ibid: 62). This point is developed more fully in the *Holy Family*:

> 'The *Jews* (like the Christians) *are* fully *politically emancipated* in various states. Both Jews and Christians are far from being *humanly* emancipated. Hence there must be a *difference* between *political* and *human* emancipation. The essence of political emancipation, i.e., of the developed, modern state, must therefore be studied. On the other hand, states which cannot yet *politically* emancipate the Jews must be rated by comparison with the perfected political state and shown to be under-developed states. That is the point of view from which the "*political* emancipation" of the Jews should have been dealt with.' (Marx, 1845)

In other words, the emancipation of Jews, Christians and all people is contingent not merely on political emancipation, which is a necessary and important progressive development, but also on human emancipation, which necessitates the abolition of capitalist social relations.

LENIN AND TROTSKY ON CONSISTENT DEMOCRACY AND 'THE JEWISH QUESTION'

In Russia and Eastern Europe at the end of the nineteenth and turn of the twentieth centuries, the existence of a Yiddish culture and language along with the conditions of violent antisemitism contributed to two forms of Jewish nationalism: a local cultural nationalism, which came to be adopted by the Jewish socialist organisation, the Bund, and a more unequivocal nationalism of political Zionism (Rodinson, 1968, 1973). Non-territorial, national cultural autonomy (NCA) was first conceptualised by the Austrian Marxist Otto Bauer. Bauer did not, incidentally, consider NCA applicable to the Jews – ironic given the Jews were a unique case of a 'non-territorial nation'. During the Second Congress of the Russian Social-Democratic Labour Party in 1903, Lenin leads an opposition (including a young Trotsky) to the Bund's call for NCA in post-revolutionary Russia. Lenin later notes that while in Austria the proposal of non-territorial NCA has largely remained 'a flight of literary fancy, which the Austrian Social-Democrats themselves have not taken seriously', in Russia it has gained political mileage (Lenin, 1903; Lenin, 1975: 30).

Lenin (1975: 27) observes that NCA is promoted as 'the "most just", "purest", most refined and civilised brand' of nationalism. But, for Lenin and Trotsky, because NCA seeks 'to separate culture from territory and economy in a society torn apart by social contradictions', such that citizens come together on 'purely personal attributes' to solve 'their "cultural" tasks (the theatre, the church, the school, and the like)' (Trotsky, 2007), it reflects 'the most refined, most absolute and most extreme nationalism' (Lenin, 1975: 26). Lenin (1975: 26) continues, the practical reality of the NCA programme is the requirement 'that every citizen registers as belonging to a particular nation', thus making affiliation to national communities akin to religious communities. Recognising the multitude of economic, social and legal bonds that bring workers of different nationalities together in a single state, Lenin regards the extrication from such bonds as historically regressive. He illustrates this point with an example from schooling: in the northern states of North America, which have a tradition of freedom and struggle against slave-ownership, 'Negro [*sic*] children attend the same schools as white children do'; while in the southern states that have a tradition of slave-ownership and racism, 'there are separate "national", or racial [...] schools for Negro children' (Lenin,

1975: 30). For Lenin, there is no question of what is to be done with the Jews, rather, he critiques the Bund's promotion of NCA as a failure to escape 'the Jewish question' by cementing national and 'racial' difference and division. Lenin (1975: 19) advances a universalist class politics of radical cultural hybridity, of which Jewish culture and history is a dynamic part:

> 'Jewish national culture is the slogan of the rabbis and the bourgeoisie, the slogan of our enemies. But there are other elements in Jewish culture and in Jewish history as a whole. Of the ten and a half million Jews in the world, somewhat over a half live in Galicia and Russia, backward and semi-barbarous countries, where the Jews are *forcibly* kept in the status of a caste. The other half lives in the civilised world, and there the Jews do not live as a segregated caste. There the great world-progressive features of Jewish culture stand clearly revealed: its internationalism, its identification with the advanced movements of the epoch (the percentage of Jews in the democratic and proletarian movements is everywhere higher than the percentage of Jews among the population).'

Lenin (1975: 7) situates the Bund's advancement of NCA as part of the development of 'a little opportunist error' (by Bauer and his naive '"forgetfulness of internationalism"') 'into a system of opportunist policy [...] *by all* the Jewish bourgeois parties and a large number of petty-bourgeois trends'. In advancing NCA for the Jewish people, he expounds, the Bund reinforces the erroneous idea of a *classless* national culture (Lenin, 1975). But, in fact, while all national cultures have rudimentary elements that are socialist and democratic, it is the bourgeois cultural elements that dominate. So, the only Marxist alternative to the national culture of 'the landlords, the clergy and the bourgeoisie' is an international, working class, radical hybrid culture that 'take[s] *from each* national culture *only* its democratic and socialist elements', but '*only* and *absolutely* in opposition to the bourgeois culture and the bourgeois nationalism of *each* nation' (Lenin, 1975: 17).

It would be a mistake to conclude that the work of Lenin advances a Marxist tradition that indiscriminately opposes national movements and nations, including the later formation of the nation state of Israel. In Lenin's (1975: 20) words, capitalism shapes the national question in two ways: one, by 'the awakening of national life and national movements, the struggle against all national oppression, and the creation of national states'; and two, by 'the development and growing frequency of international intercourse in every form, the break-down of national barriers, the creation of international unity of capital, of economic life in general, of politics, science, etc.'. Lenin (1913) insists on a consistent democracy approach to the national question:

> 'As democrats, we are irreconcilably hostile to any, however slight, oppression of any nationality and to any privileges for any nationality. As democrats, we demand the right of nations to self-determination *in the political sense* of that term (see the Programme of the R.S.D.L.P.), i.e., the right to secede. We demand unconditional *equality* for all nations in the state and the unconditional protection of the rights of every national minority. We demand broad self-government and autonomy for regions, which must be demarcated, among other terms of reference, in respect of nationality too. All these demands are obligatory for every consistent democrat, to say nothing of a socialist.'

Notably, the defence of the right to national self-determination is a 'negative' task: beyond this 'border-line […] which is often very slight' lies 'positive' work that effectively strengthens bourgeois nationalism; it is this slippage into 'positive' work that, Lenin (1975: 28) points out, the Bundists 'completely lose sight of'. In other words, defending the right of working class people to national self-determination, including their right to secede, does not stop socialists from exposing the problems of, and agitating against, bourgeois nationalism in favour of the international unity of workers in their class struggle against the bourgeoisie (Lenin, 1975). Against critics who (in line with Rosa Luxemburg's (1908–1909) *The National Question and Autonomy*) argue that Lenin's consistent democracy approach is contradictory and concedes a maximum to nationalism, Lenin (1975: 84) points out, 'in reality, the recognition of the *right of all* nations to self-determination implies the maximum of *democracy* and the minimum of nationalism'. In other words, consistent democracy on the national question is the only route out of the national question. Lenin illustrates this reasoning with the case of Sweden and Norway. Despite the territorial, economic and language bonds between Sweden and Norway, the union between the two nations was not a voluntary one, thus on the question of secession of Norway from Sweden when it arose:

'The Swedish worker could, while remaining a Social-Democrat, urge the Norwegians to vote against secession. [...] But the Swedish worker who, like the Swedish aristocracy and bourgeoisie, would deny the Norwegians the right to decide this question themselves, without the Swedes and irrespective of their will, would have been a *social-chauvinist* and a *miscreant the Social-Democratic Party could not tolerate in its ranks*. That is how clause 9 of our Party Programme should be applied. [...] And what of the Norwegian worker? Was it his [*sic*] duty, from the internationalist point of view, to vote *for* secession? Certainly not. He could have voted against secession and remained a Social-Democrat. He would have been betraying his duty as a member of the Social-Democratic Party only if he had proffered a helping hand to a Black-Hundred Swedish worker opposed to Norway's *freedom* of secession.' (Lenin, 1916)

Trotsky's (1939) summates Lenin's conclusion here: 'the relations between the Norwegian and Swedish workers improved and became closer after the disruption of the compulsory unification', that is, as a consequence of the dissolution of the compulsory union between Norway and Sweden in 1905.

A consistent democracy approach to the Palestinian-Israeli conflict means that it was and remains the duty of socialists to defend the basic democratic right of both Jewish and Palestinian people to national self-determination. The tragedy of 1948 was that one national group realised this right at the cost of another national group having their right displaced and denied. The fact that this tragedy happened does not make the right that was realised void. Furthermore, in light of British and later US imperialist support for Israel:

> 'The fact that the struggle for national liberation against one imperialist power may, under certain conditions, be utilised by another "great" power for its own, equally imperialist, aims, is just as unlikely to make the Social-Democrats refuse to recognise the right of nations to self-determination as the numerous cases of bourgeois utilisation of republican slogans for the purpose of political deception and financial plunder [...] are unlikely to make the Social-Democrats reject their republicanism.' (Lenin, 1975: 115–116)

The only consistent democracy resolution is 'two nations, two states', which concedes a maximum of democracy to both self-defined national groups and lays the conditions for a closer union between Jewish and Palestinian working class people, including the future possibility of moving beyond the national question.

Bearing in mind his death in August 1940, Trotsky's (1970) work on 'the Jewish question', written in the context of fascism and escalating violent antisemitism in Europe, is an important progression of Lenin's ideas. Trotsky comes to refer to the Jewish nation in his later writings on 'the Jewish question' – an acknowledgement that the unprecedented persecution of the Jews has made a Jewish nation a historical inevitability. He writes:

> 'During my youth I rather leaned toward the prognosis that the Jews of different countries would be assimilated and that the Jewish question would thus disappear in a quasi-automatic fashion. The historical development of the last quarter of a century has not confirmed this perspective. Decaying capitalism has everywhere swung over to an exacerbated nationalism, one part of which is anti-Semitism. [...] On the other hand the Jews of different countries have created their press and developed the Yiddish language as an instrument adapted to modern culture. One must reckon with the fact that the Jewish nation will maintain itself for an entire epoch to come.' (Trotsky, 1970: 20)

History did not encourage the disappearance of 'the Jewish question', instead, intensified nationalism and its antisemitic current fuelled 'the Jewish question', one response of which is Jewish nationalism. Trotsky (1970: 29) further recognises that a Jewish nation is not simply a historical inevitability, but is also a historical necessity for saving the Jewish people, since 'the next development of world reaction signifies with certainty the *physical extermination of the Jews*'.

He cautions that 'the Jewish question' will not be solved by capitalism:

> 'In the epoch of its rise, capitalism took the Jewish people out of the ghetto and utilized them as an instrument in its commercial expansion. Today decaying capitalist society is striving to squeeze the Jewish people from all its pores; seventeen million individuals out of the two billion populating the globe, that is,

less than one percent, can no longer find a place on our planet!' (Trotsky, 1970: 30)

Trotsky (1970: 22) foresees that a nation of Jewish people under capitalism would be 'only [...] a palliative and often even a two-edged blade'. In a future socialist society, on the basis of reciprocal understanding or something like an international workers' tribunal, he suggests, those 'dispersed Jews who would want to be reassembled in the same community' would be provided with 'a sufficiently extensive and rich spot under the sun', with 'the same possibility [...] for the Arabs, as for all other scattered nations' (Trotsky, 1970: 21). In other words: 'The very same methods of solving the Jewish question which under decaying capitalism have a utopian and reactionary character (Zionism), will, under the regime of a socialist federation, take on a real and salutary meaning' (Trotsky, 1970: 28–29).

No Marxist, and no consistent democrat even, Trotsky (1970) reasons, could object to this.

CONCLUSION

'"Real humanism" is predicated on recognising the humanity of Jews in their individuality, that is, in their empirical life, work and relationships. In defending Jewish emancipation against the restoration of the Jewish question, Marx re-affirmed the subjective right of Jews to be citizens, to be Jews, and to deal creatively, singularly, in their own way, with their Jewish origins. Real humanism is a revolt against the tyranny of provenance.' (Fine and Spencer, 2017: 40)

What has been advanced in this chapter, through a resuscitation of key writings by Rodinson, Marx, Lenin and Trotsky, is a class-based politics for political and human emancipation based on universal and radical humanism. In Rodinson's universalist critique of imperialism, colonialism and nationalism vis-à-vis Zionism and Israel, there is no singling out of Israel, Zionism and the Jews. In Marx's debate with Bruno Bauer, it is Bauer that is tied to 'the Jewish question', not Marx. It is Marx that judges the political progressiveness of any state by its political emancipation of the Jews, while recognising that true liberation lies in human emancipation from capitalism. In Lenin and Trotsky's critique of nationalism, including the cultural nationalism of the Bund, they argue for consistent democracy on the national question, that is, for the unconditional democratic right of every self-defined group of people to national self-determination. Trotsky, in the end, in a context of worsening violent antisemitism, concedes that a Jewish nation state has become historically unavoidable and a necessity to saving the Jewish people.

The Left that bemoans that it is impossible to criticise Israel without being accused of antisemitism is a Left which exceptionalises and essentialises Israel while claiming to be universal, and that denies Jewish working class people in Israel their democratic right to national self-determination under the guise of justice and redress for the Palestinians. It is a distorted and abortive universalism that demands of one designated group forfeits not required of any other group for membership of humanity. In the global struggle for political and human emancipation, and against class exploitation and oppression, the plight of the Palestinians for national liberation is a crucial one. The right to meaningful national self-determination for the Palestinians belongs alongside the same right accorded to the Israeli Jews. After all, if one day both self-defined peoples can live side by side in peace, then the prospect of a future day when both peoples live *together* becomes achievable.

Chapter 5

BUILDING AN ALLIANCE FOR HUMAN LIBERATION

'The Jewish question is not just an attitude of hostility to Jews or to those who invoke the sign of "the Jews" but a theory designed to explain the winners and losers of capitalist society. It is formulated in terms of dichotomies – the modern and the backward, the people and its enemies, the civic and the ethnic, the postnational and the national, imperialism and anti-imperialism, power and resistance, the West and the rest. In every case Jews appear as the "other of the universal": a backward people who stubbornly resist progress or an all-too-clever people who manipulate progress and hold the world in its thrall; a nation within a nation that is endemically treacherous or a nation unlike all other nations in that it is not a valid nation at all; a "settler-colonial" state in an otherwise decolonised world or a "cosmopolitan elite" with no comprehension of global responsibility.' (Fine and Spencer, 2007: 124)

'The recurrence of pain, disease, humiliation and loss of dignity, grief, and care for those one loves can all contribute to an abstract sense of a human similarity powerful enough to make solidarities based on cultural particularity appear suddenly trivial.' (Gilroy, 2000: 17)

The goal of political and human emancipation, and, furthermore, of saving ourselves as a species, other species and planet Earth, requires a recognition that we share our existence, we need one another, and (as human beings) we are not divided by inherent differences that prevent us from organising together. The human condition in its most basic experiences of love, suffering and grief ought to strip away the hold of cultural differences that impede our ability to connect with others. Yet, a significant tendency of the Left, in thinking that it is in a class war against an all-powerful and omnipresent Zionism, is actually waging a cultural war against the Jews. The Left's 'Jewish question' cuts against any genuine sense that we are all fundamentally similar and worthy of solidarity by making an enemy Other of the Jew.

The Left's casting of the Palestinian-Israeli conflict through a racialised identity script of 'the Jews' and 'the Palestinians' as villains and victims is actually a divisive identity politics masquerading as inclusive universalist politics. As soon as progressive movements for human liberation uncritically embrace identity politics (and therein cultural essentialism), they become self-defeating. After all, racism and nationalism are also forms of identity politics premised on the idea of intrinsic differences. I proceed to present the work of the scholars Cornel West and Henry Louis Gates, Jr. on black antisemitism and its impediment to an alliance of black and Jewish people in the struggle against racism. I do so because their writings are relevant in challenging both essentialist ideas in anti-racist politics and a Left that hails the fight against anti-black racism while failing to see anti-Jewish racism in its ideological midst.

LESSONS FROM WEST AND GATES ON BLACK ANTISEMITISM

The writings of Cornel West and Henry Louis Gates, Jr. on the rising prevalence of black antisemitism in the United States are a noteworthy example of an intellectual commitment to a full and inclusive front in the fight against oppression and exploitation. In confronting the issue of antisemitism in black anti-racist politics, both recognise antisemitism as a grave impediment in the fight against anti-black racism. Moreover, both understand anti-Jewish racism as the bedfellow of anti-black racism, past and present. Specifically, West provides a fascinating analysis of the causes of black antisemitic ideas, some of which have resonance for comprehending anti-Jewish racism on the Left more generally. And Gates explores the cultural essentialism of black anti-semitism – offering an insight into how movements for political liberation jeopardise their goal by making Others out of Others. In sum, the work of West and Gates, in challenging racism from within a culturally defined group of people who themselves are victims of racism, provide an important discussion point for those on the Left who, in contrast, respond to the accusation of anti-Jewish racism with derision.

In 'On Black-Jewish Relations', West (1994: 147) notes the intersectionality of the Palestinian-Israeli conflict in Jewish and black identification and the implications of this for anti-racist alliance and struggle:

> 'Without a sympathetic understanding of the deep historic sources of Jewish fears and anxieties about group survival, blacks will not grasp the visceral attachment of most Jews to Israel. Similarly, without a candid acknowledgment of blacks' status as permanent underdogs in American society, Jews will not comprehend what the symbolic predicament and literal plight of Palestinians in Israel means to blacks.'

Two factors, he argues, solidified the conflicting directions of Jewish and black identity: the rise of the Israeli Right in government from 1977 onwards and the ascendency of black nationalism in the United States during the 1980s. The support of mainstream US Jewish organisations for the oppressive policies of the Israeli governments of Begin and Shamir, and the conspiratorial targeting of Jewish power by US black nationalist leaders like Leonard Jeffries and Louis Farrakhan, have set Jew and black apart (West, 1994).

West (1994) provides five defining features of black antisemitism. The first, 'anti-whitism': Jewish people are seen to be complicit in racism and to be the beneficiaries of white privilege, and, with this visible skin privilege (alongside a generally perceived higher socio-economic position in US society), Jews are cast as 'the public face of oppression for the black community' (ibid: 150). Anti-whitism, West (1994) states, denies the history of antisemitism. Second is the different moral standard that is held of Jewish people in comparison to the rest of the white population due to the history of antisemitism. Consequently, 'the charge of "betrayal"', in which 'many stock Christian anti-Semitic narratives' re-surface, is made in response to the public profile of US Jewish neoconservatism (West, 1994: 150). The third feature is 'underdog resentment and envy' at the underdog who is seen to have succeeded in US society, which slides into myths of Jewish uniformity and the idea of 'favouritism and nepotism among Jews', and constructs the view that Jews represent an obstacle rather than a partnership in the struggle for racial justice (ibid: 151). West (1994: 151) explains the upsurge of black antisemitism by its two final features: the identification of the Palestinian-Israeli conflict with the US Jewish 'establishment' and the 'visible *conservative* Jewish opposition to what is perceived to be a major means of black progress [...] affirmative action'. As he puts it, while 'principled critiques of US foreign policy in the Middle East, of Israeli denigration of Palestinians, or attacks on affirmative action *transcend* anti-Semitic sensibilities', 'vulgar critiques do not':

> 'And in the rhetoric of a Louis Farrakhan or a Leonard Jeffries, whose audiences rightly hunger for black self-respect and oppose black degradation, these critiques misdirect progressive black energies arrayed against unaccountable corporate power and antiblack racism, steering them instead *toward* Jewish elites and antiblack conspiracies in Jewish America. This displacement is disturbing not

only because it is analytically and morally wrong; it also discourages any effective alliances across races.' (West, 1994: 151–152)

In sum, the intersection of the Palestinian-Israeli conflict with black nationalism sets apart people who are committed to anti-racism, because the political critique of the repressive policies and practices of the Israeli state and military against the Palestinians is turned into antisemitic conspiratorial critique against the Jews in general.

West's (1994) definition of black antisemitism, although specific to black nationalism, also connects with an understanding of anti-Jewish racism on the Left: the Palestinian-Israeli conflict is the means by which all Jewish people are judged, while the historical Jewish experience of genocidal antisemitism that fuels a 'visceral attachment' (147) to Israel is ignored; on the other hand, because of the Holocaust, Jewish people are held to account by a higher moral standard than other people; and Jews present as 'white' and as having 'white skin privilege', so are seen to escape racism and to be racist. In a podcast for the United States Holocaust Memorial Museum, West (2007) offers the following stark warning:

'Part of the bourgeois-ossification of American Jewry has to do with the whitening of Jews in the eyes of those on the outside of the mainstream. There's no doubt about that. But I think on the other hand, even if some Jews do believe that they're white, I think that they're duped. I think that antisemitism has proven itself to be a powerful force in nearly every post of Western civilization where Christianity has a presence. And so even as a Christian, I say continually to my Jewish brothers and sisters: don't believe the hype about your full scale assimilation and integration into a mainstream. It only takes an event or two for a certain kind of anti-Jewish, antisemitic sensibility to surface in places that you would be surprised.'

The tendency in the anti-racist imagination to see, and only see, the outward markers of 'race', namely, racism targeted against people with dark-toned skin, forgets that in the history of racism, the markers of 'race' were much more variable, including the racialisation of the Jewish Other's invisibility. Furthermore, in the history of racism, 'racial' antisemitism (or anti-Jewish racism) was not a clean break from religious antisemitism, but rather a reworking of former representations of the Other into a new racist discourse. Contemporary anti-Jewish racism absorbs and reconfigures past ideas of the Jews, both from the history and pre-history of racism. The enemy Jew of today is the Jew of the uniquely threatening nation, while the enemy Jew of the past was the Jew of the uniquely threatening nation within the nation.

In 'The Uses of Anti-Semitism', originally an opinion piece in *The New York Times* titled 'Black Demagogues and Pseudo-Scholars' (1992), Gates (1994) calls out a rising wave of black antisemitism in books popular within the Afrocentric movement that have been given academic credibility. Notably, in this respect, is *The Iceman Inheritance: Prehistoric Sources of Western Man's Racism, Sexism, and Aggression* by Michael Bradley, which claims that the exceptional viciousness of white people is a consequence of their descent from brutish Neanderthals: 'More to the point, it speculates that the Jews may have been the "'purest' and oldest Neanderthal-Caucasoids," the iciest of the ice people: hence ([Bradley] explains) the singularly odious character of ancient Jewish culture' (Gates, 1994: 218).

Gates (1994) condemns the endorsement and promotion of this book by black academics. He also observes the legitimisation of rising black antisemitism by university campus speakers and publications, providing two examples. The first, the black newspaper *Nommo* at the University of California, Los Angeles, which defended the importance of the *Protocols of the Elders of Zion*, and, in response to criticism for doing so, published an article titled 'Anti-Semitic? Ridiculous – Chill'. And a speech given at Harvard University by the national youth representative of the Nation of Islam, which 'neatly annexed environmentalism to anti-Semitism' by blaming Jews for the destruction of the ozone layer (Gates, 1994: 219).

The bible of contemporary black antisemitism, Gates (1994) suggests, is *The Secret Relationship Between Blacks and Jews*, which was published by the Nation of Islam. He defines this book as 'one of the most sophisticated instances of hate literature yet compiled', and elaborates:

'It charges that the Jews were in fact "key operatives" in the historic crime of slavery, playing an "inordinate" and "disproportionate" role and "carv[ing] out for themselves a monumental culpability in slavery – and the black holocaust." And among significant sectors of the black community, this brief has become a credo of a new philosophy of black self-affirmation. To be sure, the book massively misrepresents the historical record, largely through a process of cunningly selective quotations of often reputable sources. But its authors could be confident that few of its readers would go to the trouble of actually hunting down the works cited. For if readers actually did so, they might discover a rather different picture. They might find out – from the book's own vaunted authorities – that, for example, of all the African slaves imported into the New World, American Jewish merchants accounted for less than 2 percent, a finding sharply at odds with the Nation's claim of Jewish "predominance" in this traffic. They might find out that, in the domestic trade, it appears that all of the Jewish slave traders *combined* bought and sold fewer slaves than the single gentile firm of Franklin and Armfield. In short, they might learn what the historian Harold Brackman has documented at length: that the book's repeated insistence that the Jews dominated the slave trade depends on an unscrupulous distortion of the historic record. But the most ominous words in the book are found on the cover: "volume one." More have been promised, carrying on the saga of Jewish iniquity to the present day.' (Gates, 1994: 219–220)

The wider significance of this classic text of black antisemitism is demonstrated by the absorption of its idea that Jews were the chief financiers of the slave trade into the ideological milieu of the Left (see, for example: BBC, 2016).

Worse than the 'shoddy [...] scholarship' of books like *The Iceman Inheritance* and *The Secret Relationship*, Gates (1994: 220) contends, is 'the tacit conviction that culpability is heritable': 'For it suggests a doctrine of racial continuity, in which the racial evil of a people is merely manifest (rather than constituted) by their historical misdeeds. The reported misdeeds are thus the *signs* of an essential nature that is evil.'

Furthermore, Gates (1994: 221) reveals the dangerous intention of black nationalist leaders like Louis Farrakhan to 'convert a relation of friendship, alliance, and uplift into one of enmity, distrust, and hatred'. Black antisemitism helps black nationalist politics win over people who might otherwise be drawn to a politics from the civil rights movement that fights against anti-black and anti-Jewish racisms together. 'Why target the Jews?', Gates (1994: 221) expands:

'The answer requires us to go beyond the usual shibboleths about bigotry and view the matter, from the demagogue's perspective, strategically: as the bid of one black elite to supplant another. It requires me, in short, to see anti-Semitism as a weapon in the raging battle of who will speak for black America: those who have sought common cause with others, or those who preach a barricaded withdrawal into racial authenticity.'

By making enemies of the Jews, the black nationalist 'apostles of hate' advance 'ethnic isolationism' and thus consolidate their own power

(Gates, 1994: 221). As such, for these 'tacticians' of a new black anti-semitism, 'the original sin of American Jews' was not 'their involvement – truly "inordinate," truly "disproportionate" [...] in slavery, but in the front ranks of the civil rights struggle' (ibid: 222). Here Gates counterposes the history of black-Jewish alliance in the US civil rights movement (contingent on the recognition of universal commonality) with black identity politics that barricades and withdraws black America into the seeming comfort of racial authenticity and cultural essentialism.

The scapegoating of Jewish people, Gates (1994: 228) spells out, 'hurts black people, through the politics of distraction and distortion':

> 'Objectively speaking, black anti-Semitism isn't primarily a Jewish problem, it's a black problem. In the words of the formidable critic and activist Barbara Smith, "We don't oppose anti-Semitism because we owe something to Jewish people, but because we owe something very basic to ourselves."'

Likewise, the Left must oppose anti-Jewish racism not because we owe something specifically to Jewish people, but because we owe something very basic to ourselves and our sense of what it means to be human.

CONCLUSION

The Left's culture war against the Jews effectively preserves a divided humanity by locking it into a duel. We have to be able to recognise our overriding commonality and strive for a radical universalism where no 'harmful Other' is constructed and excluded from humanity, and where there is no designated test for any individual of any demarcated group to prove their exceptionality and worthiness of solidarity and belonging. After all, the tragedy of casting out Jews from the anti-racist imagination is that the dream of freedom is subsequently lost for everyone.

When I first came across the Nazi propaganda image of 'Jonny' – a caricature of a prominent black jazz musician mutated into a monkey and wearing the Star of David – I was struck by its illustration of how different oppressive ideas intersect. This image formed part of a wider culture war by Nazi Germany against the Weimer Republic years. In Nazi discourse, the Weimer Republic represented the pollution and degeneration of German culture by 'non-Aryan' and 'anti-nationalist' elements. *Entartete Musik* was the name of a Nazi propaganda exhibition in Dusseldorf on 24 May 1938, which showcased the work of composers and musicologists that the National Socialist government had banned as 'entartete', that is, degenerate and decadent (Berg, 2013). The brochure for the exhibition carried on its title page this caricature of 'Jonny'. The exhibition was part of a wider reaction against the everyday life of the Weimer Republic's golden years, which made threatening Others out of the socially constructed differences of 'race', sex, gender, and sexuality, including the fear of sexual excess and transgression represented by the Republic's modern art and avant-garde literary scenes, gay bars, and '"manly women"' (Mosse, 1985: xx). The most significant Others of *Entartete Musik* were the Jewish writers and composers influenced by jazz, which was scorned 'nigger [*sic*] music' (cited in Berg, 2013). In the opening speech to the exhibition, the Nazi official, Hans Severus Ziegler, stated that the works on show constituted 'an effigy of wickedness – an effigy of arrogant Jewish impudence and complete spiritual insipidness' (cited in Berg, 2013). 'Jonny' is a reminder for the present day of what Gates (2020) powerfully states are the 'two hideous demons' that 'slumber under the floorboards of Western culture: anti-Semitism and anti-Black racism', which 'can erupt through those floorboards at any time.'

Chapter 6
CONCLUSION

In the anti-racist imagination, Jewish people as actual and potential victims of racism have been banished as a consequence of the racialisation of 'the Jews' vis-à-vis Zionism and Israel as not just white and privileged, but ultra-white and uber-privileged, so glaringly white, in fact, that their racist global power and reach is invisible to the naked eye. A potent mix of 'the Jewish question' and a colonial model of racism has created both a blind spot and an exclusion in anti-racist ideology that not only fails to recognise antisemitism but reacts to the cries of antisemitism with contempt and revenge. The result is the disconnection of antisemitism from racism, or, at best, the relegation of antisemitism to the past, and the equation of Zionism as racism's colonial past, present and future that must be redressed through the total elimination of Israel. Accordingly, the person that identifies as Jewish and who speaks out against anti-Jewish racism on the Left is accused of making a false allegation with the sly motivation to impede pro-Palestinian solidarity and fortify an expansionist, racist and colonialist Israel. Furthermore, this person feels obliged to state their pro-Palestinian and anti-Zionist beliefs in a futile bid to have their experience of racism heard and legitimised. No other person who cries 'racism!' – other than the one who is Jewish – is treated in such a way.

I began *Outcast* with a quote from Hannah Arendt's essay, 'Between Pariah and Parvenu', because of its resonance with contemporary leftist racialisation of 'the Jew'. In this essay, Arendt (1976) observes that all advocates of emancipation considered Jewish emancipation in terms of assimilation, which meant that 'the Jewish question' was approached only in its social aspect. She states:

> 'It has been one of the most unfortunate facts in the history of the Jewish people that only its enemies, and almost never its friends, understood that the Jewish question was a political one. The defenders of emancipation tended to present the problem as one of "education," a concept which originally applied to Jews as well as non-Jews. It was taken for granted that the vanguard in both camps would consist of specially "educated," tolerant, cultured persons. It followed, of course, that the particularly tolerant, educated and cultured non-Jews could be bothered socially only with exceptionally educated Jews. As a matter of course, the demand, among the educated, for the abolition of prejudice was very quickly to become a rather one-sided affair, until only the Jews, finally, were urged to educate themselves.' (Arendt, 1976: 56–57)

The historical demand that ordinary Jews, who cling to their reactionary non-national nation, educate themselves to become exceptional Jews, reverberates on the present-day Left in the demand that ordinary Jews break from the illegitimate nation state of Israel and educate themselves into becoming exceptional individual Jews. Moreover, not only are the Jews (then and now) confronted with the 'demoralising demand' to be exceptions to the Jews in general, they are also expected to be 'exceptional specimens of humanity' (Arendt, 1976: 58). It is in this sense that Arendt (1976) states that 'the Jewish question' of the Enlightenment was a social rather than a political question. This can still be seen on the Left, since it is the Jews, and the Jews alone, who must be withdrawn from their political right to national self-determination, while socially demonstrating their educated insight and determination to accord this same right, which must be denied to them, to the Palestinians. The anti-Zionist Jew who fights for a resolution to the Palestinian-Israeli conflict on the basis of the right to national self-determination for both the Palestinians and the Israeli Jews is not good enough. 'From the river to the sea, Palestine will be free!', the Jew must cry, to become an exceptional Jew and an exceptional specimen of humanity. The Left has, of course, its exceptional Jews, who insist that antisemitism does not exist on the Left except as a fabricated accusation to silence progressive voices criticising Israel, and who claim that Zionism is a threat to world peace and that Israel has to be destroyed. Indeed, the Left's exceptional Jews are proof, one is told, that there is no anti-Jewish racism on the Left – remember, 'we are not hostile to Jews as Jews' – such is the fetish of politicised and racialised identities to claim authenticity and speak the truth.

The foremost scholar that I have drawn upon in *Outcast* for understanding the idea of 'race', the process of racialisation that creates this idea in the first place, the common-sense ideology of racism, and the basic problem with reifying 'race' and framing enquiry into racism through a colonial model, especially for the question of antisemitism and Zionism, is Professor Robert Miles. It is not incidental that when he was asked in an interview whether his work was impeded by the racialisation of him by others in the field of the study of racism as 'white', he replied: 'I was involved in debates at times in which my position was ruled out of court because I was a "white" man' (cited in Ashe and McGeever, 2011: 2015). Racialised identities are given a fixed reality and power on the activist and academic Left which cements rather transcends division, with the implicit belief that, for example, only black and brown people can know what racism is, and white Jews cannot experience real racism. However, as Miles (1993) powerfully elucidates, given Marxism sees all social relationships as socially constructed and reproduced through specific class agencies and conditions of existence, then there should be no space for ideological concepts that claim (implicitly or explicitly) the opposite. As such, there should be no Marxist, leftist or critical theory of 'race', which effectively makes 'race' real, instead there should be theories that deconstruct the idea of 'race' to reveal the role of human signification and its exclusionary consequences.

The Jewish nation state and its allies have become *the* Other and *the* opprobrium of leftist thought. Indeed, the Left's 'Jewish question' and colonial model of racism represent a form of racialised identity politics that bypasses universal class politics and solidarity: post-1967, Palestine has become a left credential. To hang or wave the Palestinian flag and to wear the Palestinian keffiyeh is an expression of personal and political identity with the ultimate victim of the ultimate oppressor. Through the intersecting lenses of 'white versus black', 'settler versus native' and 'harmful Zionist Jew versus Palestinian victim', there is no recognition that class differentiation cuts across these dichotomies. The Israeli Jewish working class becomes non-existent, since it is assumed to subsume itself blindly into the ruling class, never to be won over to left-wing ideas. And the Palestinian working class is located in victimhood rather than agency. Palestinians and Israelis are rarely regarded as part of societies with differing and conflicting class interests, concerns, allegiances and politics. It is not the task of the anti-racist to invert and re-essentialise the racist imagination, instead, the undertaking is to recognise racism as a common-sense ideology that must be debated and overcome with politically progressive ideas. And yet, there is an anti-racist imagination that responds to the racist depiction of Palestinians as barbaric terrorists through its own racialisation of Israeli Jews as ethnic cleansers, who are so morally depraved that they have channelled their victimhood from the Nazi concentration camps into a cutting-edge ability to persecute and execute genocide in their own concentration camps. Zionism, Israel and all Jews connected with either, are signified, morally condemned and accordingly placed outside the boundaries of civilisation. In essence, anti-Jewish racism on the Left is a reactionary anti-capitalism, anti-colonialism, anti-imperialism and anti-racism, because it fuses, fixes and makes innate socially constructed difference ('Zionism', 'Israel' and 'Jews') with capitalism.

Over the years on the activist and academic Left, I have frequently heard or read the assertion that Zionism is a particularly reprehensible racism and Israel is a uniquely illegitimate nation state. This obsession with Israel (which translates the Palestinian-Israeli conflict as exceptional, rather than comparable) has always seemed to me incongruent with a universalist politics. As despicable as the policies and actions of the Israeli state against the Palestinians are, and as much as one might despair at the lack of a mass oppositional movement inside Israel, neither diminishes the harm also done to humanity by other despicable states, with the apparent acquiescence of their populations, or the need to build grassroots solidarity and resistance across all borders and ethnically self-defined groups of people. The genocides committed by states in recent times, notably, Russia in Chechnya and Ukraine, Sudan in the Darfur region, Sri Lanka on the Tamils, China on the Uyghurs, Saudi Arabia and the United Arab Emirates in the Yemen, the Islamic State on Christians, Shia Muslims and Yazidis, and Myanmar on the Rohingya, simply do not consume the energies of the Left like Israel on Palestine. As much as this Left complains that Israel monopolises victimhood through a Holocaust industry that silences criticism of Israel, this Left monopolies Israel as the world's evil villain.

One of my earliest encounters with the Socialist Workers' Party, as a nineteen-year-old, brought me to the realisation that 'Zionist!' was a *slur* thrown at me for my position on the Palestinian-Israeli conflict (of two nations, two states). This slur, it felt, carried a similar bitterness to the slur 'Paki!' that I was familiar with from childhood experiences of racism. Indeed, both slurs intended to demean me as *a lesser human being*. As a new activist on the Left, I quickly learned that I was no longer a 'Paki', I was now a 'Zionist'. I also realised that outside of left-wing meetings and demonstrations, I was still nonetheless a 'Paki'. As the years have passed, it has become clearer to me that on this Left, despite being a 'Zionist', because I am a 'Paki', I have experienced an immunity not shared with my 'white' comrades from being called, outright, a racist. Perhaps now, however, as the author of this book, the immunity will fade. I have also reflected on the irony of these slurs, 'Paki' and 'Zionist', given my family history in the divided state of the Punjab of a partitioned India and Pakistan. Both Israel and Pakistan were nation states founded on religious national identities, in the courtship of British imperialism, in the death throes of the British Empire, and to the exclusion, exile and death of other human beings. To me, there is no one-of-a-kind, stand-alone and top-of-the-league-table regressive nation state, warranting (unlike any other nation state) immediate dissolution. As much as there is specificity on the question of Israel and the Palestinian-Israeli conflict, such specificity does not override the historically familiar problems that are represented here and which we collectively need to overcome everywhere.

Given the tendency of many leftists to morally doom Zionism, Israel and associated Jews as 'racist!', it is worth emphasising that the approach in *Outcast* to the idea of 'race' and the common-sense ideology of racism means that such leftists should not likewise be condemned as racist, rather it is their reactionary and racist ideas which must be challenged. What is required, and what is desperately lacking, in the activist and academic Left, are genuinely open spaces for discussion and debate on this issue. The bind of the Jew, to be damned as an ordinary Jew, or to be permitted onto the Left as an exceptional Jew, is indicative of the closure of thought on the Palestinian-Israeli conflict and the prison house of 'the Jewish question'. Many of the left-wing activists and academics I want an interlocution with will no doubt dismiss *Outcast* as soft on Zionism and Israel, and as not saying enough about the deplorable conditions of existence and treatment of the Palestinians. *Outcast* will undoubtedly be dismissed as being soft on racism – the real racism against the Palestinians. This dismissal is a core symptom of the problem that I have sought to expose and explain.

There is no debate here about who succeeded and who lost in 1948. There is no debate about who is the oppressor state and who is, fundamentally, the injured party. There is no debate about whether Israel as a nation state is racist and colonialist. The issue is *how* these 'truths' are comprehended. The challenge I pose to much of the Left is: why do you treat the Jewish person who raises concern of anti-Jewish racism in your ranks so dismissively and contemptuously? Can you not recognise both the weaponisation of antisemitism and the reality of antisemitism? To paraphrase Fine and Spencer (2017): Jews were never the problem, and they are not the problem now; the issue is the Left's entrapment in 'the Jewish question' and the anti-Jewish racism which creates this question in the first place. To place a mirror to the Left that sees Jews as the problem, and to get this Left to look at itself, is the only means through which a real and radical universalism can prevail. In sum, the Left needs to relinquish the idea of the ordinary and exceptional Jew to see our basic commonality as human beings, and, from there, rebuild a vision of political and human emancipation. Anti-Jewish racism on the Left is not simply a betrayal to Jewish people, it reflects a tragic inability to realise a future of full democracy and coexistence for all.

ACKNOWLEDGEMENTS

I am incredibly grateful to the team at No Pasaran Media for the opportunity, support and resources to write this book. The book has been in my head for many years, but it would not have become a reality without No Pasaran. Furthermore, from the outset, the team has given me full academic freedom; given the multiple tides *Outcast* rides against, this has been a cathartic intellectual opening which I have savoured.

My comrade Daniel Randall, author of No Pasaran's *Confronting Antisemitism on the Left: Arguments for Socialists*, also deserves a special acknowledgement. Daniel's promotion of my own ideas on the issue of antisemitism on the Left no doubt brought me to the attention of the publishers. Daniel is, in a Gramscian sense, an important and inspiring organic intellectual on the Left, and has been a critical interlocutor in my own political development.

The earliest drafts of this book were, I am sure, infuriating to read: I knew what I wanted to say but the narrative had yet to surface. My gratitude then to my comrade Paul Hampton, who ploughed through the early chapter drafts trying to piece it all together, and who provided me with swift and punchy feedback. His steer was crucial to me getting there. My comrades and friends Karen Escott and Jol Miskin generously committed their time too to reading chapter drafts and their feedback was significant in the book becoming more accessible.

The structural editor, Robert Philpot, deserves a special mention. Robert really understood what the narrative was and how to execute it. It was a pleasure to have his insight and input.

A more general acknowledgement is due to my comrades in Workers' Liberty: the crucible of my politics on the Palestinian-Israeli conflict and the home to the debate and development of my ideas on emancipatory politics.

Finally, deep gratitude goes to my partner, Louisa Cadman. Louisa provided both intellectual labour and domestic labour to enable this book to happen. As the co-parent to our two young children, she read and gave feedback on the chapter drafts (with her usual impressive ability to help draw out my line of argument) and she provided me with vital time to write while she cared for our family. Louisa recognised just how much this book project meant to me and consistently went the extra mile to support its fruition. Thank you.

It goes without saying, any errors in this book are mine and mine alone.

REFERENCES

Chapter 1

Arendt, Hannah (1976) *The Origins of Totalitarianism*, A Harvest Book: London.

Ashe, Stephen D. and Brendan McGeever (2011) 'Marxism, racism and the construction of "race" as a social and political relation: an interview with Professor Robert Miles', *Ethnic and Racial Studies* 34(12), 2009–2026.

Beckett, Andy (2002) '"It's water on stone, in the end the stone wears out"', *Guardian*, https://www.theguardian.com/education/2002/dec/12/highereducation.uk, last accessed 20 February 2022.

Brah, Avtar (1996) *Cartographies of Diaspora: Contesting identities*, Routledge: London.

Brown, Wendy (1995) *States of Injury: power and freedom in late modernity*, Princeton University Press: Princeton, NJ.

Cadman, Louisa (2006) 'A genealogy of (bio)political contestation during the reform of the Mental Health Act 1983 in England and Wales', DPhil, University of Sheffield: Sheffield.

Drury, Colin (2019) 'Hong Kong protests: Clashes in Sheffield as rival groups stand off in city centre', *Independent*, https://www.independent.co.uk/news/uk/home-news/hong-kong-protests-latest-sheffield-clashes-bottles-thrown-chinese-students-a9135186.html, last accessed 20 February 2022.

Engels, Frederick (1998) 'Letter to Joseph Bloch', in John Storey (editor) *Cultural Theory and Popular Culture: A Reader*, Prentice Hall: London, 71–72.

Fine, Robert and Philip Spencer (2017) *Antisemitism and the left: On the return of the Jewish question*, Manchester University Press: Manchester.

Finkelstein, Norman (2015) 'Is there a rise in anti-Semitism in Europe?', YouTube, https://youtu.be/iDSP9lmMQzg, last accessed 27 April 2021.

Gilroy, Paul (2000) *Against Race: Imagining Political Culture beyond the Color Line*, The Belknap Press of Harvard University: Cambridge, Massachusetts.

Gordon, Neve (2018) 'The "New Anti-Semitism"', *London Review of Books*, https://www.lrb.co.uk/the-paper/v40/n01/neve-gordon/the-new-anti-semitism, last accessed 16 February 2022.

Hirsh, David (2018) *Contemporary Left Antisemitism*, Routledge: London.

Kaur, Harmeet (2021) 'A Sikh man's murder at a gas station revealed another tragedy of 9/11', CNN, https://edition.cnn.com/interactive/2021/09/us/balbir-singh-sodhi-9-11-cec/, last accessed 16 February 2022.

Klug, Brian (2013) 'What Do We Mean When We Say "Antisemitism": Echoes of shattering glass', *Proceedings/International conference*, https://www.jmberlin.de/sites/default/files/antisemitism-in-europe-today_2-klug.pdf, last accessed 16 February 2022.

Marx, Karl (1965) *The German Ideology*, International Publishers: New York.

Miller, David (2021) 'Building the Campaign for Free Speech conference, Feb 13 2021 – part 1', YouTube, https://youtu.be/oYc_dO-6Ua8, last accessed 11 April 2022.

Miller, David (2020) 'Campaign for Free Speech! With Norman Finkelstein, Tariq Ali, Jackie Walker and others', YouTube, https://

www.youtube.com/watch?v=MSjlMHNkEWg, last accessed 11 April 2022.

O'Loughlin, John (2004) 'Academic openness, boycotts and journal policy', *Political Geography* 23(6), 641–643.

Pappé, Ilan (2019) 'Socialism 101: Anti-Zionism is not antisemitism – Ilan Pappé', YouTube, https://www.youtube.com/watch?v=c__G_ in2Dyo, last accessed 11 April 2022.

Shepherd, Jessica (2009) 'Lecturers vote to boycott Israeli universities', *Guardian*, https://www.theguardian.com/education/2009/may/27/lecturers-vote-boycott, last accessed 20 February 2022.

Slater, David (2004) 'Editorial comment: academic politics and Israel/Palestine', *Political Geography* 23(6), 645–646.

Storey, David (2005) 'Academic boycotts, activism and the academy', *Political Geography* 24(8), 992–997.

Support David Miller (2021) 'Educators and researchers in support of Professor Miller', *Support David Miller*, https://supportmiller.org/educators-and-researchers, last accessed 11 April 2022.

SWP TV (2017) 'Zionism, antisemitism and the left today – John Rose, Brian Klug & Rob Ferguson', Socialist Workers' Party Marxism Festival, https://youtu.be/XhkkpKlSvH4, last accessed 16 February 2022.

UCU Hallam (2021) 'SHU UCU Special Branch Meeting 17 November 2021', UCU Hallam, https://ucuhallam.org/wp-content/uploads/2021/12/17-Nov-21-UCU-SHU-Branch-minutes.pdf, last accessed 20 February 2022.

Waterman, Stanley (2004) 'Letter to the editor: True exchanges or thought crime?', *Political Geography* 24(8), 998–1001.

Yiftachel, Oren and As'ad Ghanem (2004) 'Understanding "ethnocratic" regimes: the politics of seizing contested territories', *Political Geography* 23(6), 647–676.

Chapter 2

Back, Les and John Solomos (editors) (2000) *Theories of Race and Racism: A Reader*, Routledge: London.

Barker, Anthony J. (1978) *The African Link: British Attitudes to the Negro in the Era of the Atlantic Slave Trade, 1550–1807*, Frank Cass: London.

Bauman, Zygmunt (2000) 'Modernity, Racism, Extermination', in Back, Les and John Solomos (editors) *Theories of Race and Racism: A Reader*, Routledge: London, 212–228.

Bauman, Zygmunt (1989) *Modernity and the Holocaust*, Polity Press: Cambridge.

Blauner, Robert (1969) 'Internal Colonialism and Ghetto Revolt', *Social Problems* 16(4), 393–408.

Cohen, Philip (1988) 'The Perversions of Inheritance: Studies in the Making of Multi-Racist Britain', in Philip Cohen and Harwant S. Bains (editors) *Multi-Racist Britain*, Macmillan: London, 9–118.

Cousin, Glynis and Robert Fine (2012) 'A Common Cause: Reconnecting the study of racism and antisemitism', *European Societies* 14(2), 166–185.

Gilroy, Paul (1998) 'Race ends here', *Ethnic and Racial Studies* 21(5), 838–847.

Gramsci, Antonio (1971) *Selections from Prison Notebooks*, Lawrence and Wishart: London.

Guillaumin, Colette (1999) '"I Know it's Not Nice, But…" The Changing Face of "Race"', in Rodolfo D. Torres, Louis F. Mirón and Jonathan Xavier Inda (editors) *Race, Identity and Citizenship: A Reader*, Blackwell: Oxford, 39–46.

Miles, Robert and Malcolm Brown (2003) *Racism* (Second edition), Routledge: London.

Miles, Robert and Rodolfo D. Torres (1999) 'Does "Race" Matter? Transatlantic Perspectives on Racism after "Race Relations"', in Rodolfo D. Torres, Louis F. Mirón and Jonathan Xavier Inda (editors) *Race, Identity and Citizenship: A Reader*, Blackwell: Oxford, 19–38.

Miles, Robert (1993) *Racism after 'race relations'*, Routledge: London.

Miles, Robert (1989) *Racism*, Routledge: London.

Miles, Robert (1987) 'Recent Marxist Theories of Nationalism and the Issue of Racism', *The British Journal of Sociology* 38(1), 24–43.

Miles, Robert (1984) 'Marxism versus the sociology of "race relations"?', *Ethnic and Racial Studies* 7(2), 217–237.

Mosse, George L. (2000) 'The Jews: Myth and Counter-Myth', in Back, Les and John Solomos (editors) *Theories of Race and Racism: A Reader*, Routledge: London, 195–205.

Mosse, George L. (1985) *Toward the Final Solution: A History of European Racism*, The University of Wisconsin Press: Wisconsin.

Said, Edward (1995) *Orientalism*, Penguin Books: London.

Thomas, James M. (2010) 'The racial formation of medieval Jews: a challenge to the field', *Ethnic and Racial Studies* 33(10), 1737–1755.

Werbner, Pnina (2013) 'Folk devils and racist imaginaries in a global prism: Islamophobia and anti-Semitism in the twenty-first century', *Ethnic and Racial Studies* 36(3), 450–467.

Wolfe, Patrick (2016) *Traces of History: Elementary Structures of Race*, Verso: London.

Zia-Ebrahimi, Reza (2018) 'When the Elders of Zion relocated to Eurabia: conspiratorial racialization in antisemitism and Islamophobia', *Patterns of Prejudice* 52(4), 314–337.

Chapter 3

Anderson, Perry (2000) 'Renewals', *New Left Review* 1, 5–24.

Ashcroft, Bill and Pal Ahluwalia (2001) *Edward Said*, Routledge: London.

Bashir, Bashir and Rachel Busbridge (2019) 'The Politics of Decolonisation and Bi-Nationalism in Israel/Palestine', *Political Studies* 67(2), 388–405.

Bassi, Camila (2011) 'The Inane Politics of Tony Cliff', *The Journal for the Study of Antisemitism* 3(2), 725–734.

Buhle, Paul (1991) *Marxism in the United States: Remapping the History of the American Left*, Verso: London.

Busbridge, Rachel (2018) 'Israel-Palestine and the Settler Colonial "Turn": From Interpretation to Decolonization', *Theory, Culture & Society* 35(1), 91–115.

Caksu, Ali (2020) 'Islamophobia, Chinese Style: Total Internment of Uyghur Muslims by the People's Republic of China', *Islamophobia Studies Journal* 5(2), 176–198.

Cohen, Ben (2004) *A Discourse of Delegitimisation: The British Left and the Jews*, https://archive.jpr.org.uk/download?id=2228, last accessed 6 July 2022.

Crooke, Stan (2002) 'The Stalinist roots of "left anti-Zionism"', in Clive Bradley, Stan Crooke and Sean Matgamna *Two nations, two states: Socialists and Israel/Palestine*, Upstream Press: London.

Dalsheim, Joyce (2013) 'Anachronism and Morality: Israeli Settlement, Palestinian Nationalism, and Human Liberation', *Theory, Culture & Society* 30(3), 29–60.

Dalsheim, Joyce (2011) *Unsettling Gaza: Secular Liberalism, Radical Religion, and the Israeli Settlement Project*, Oxford University Press: Oxford.

Falah, Ghazi (2004) 'Truth at War and Naming the Intolerable in Palestine', *Antipode* 36(4), 596–600.

Falah, Ghazi (2003) 'Dynamics and patterns of the shrinking of Arab lands in Palestine', *Political Geography* 22(2), 179–209.

Falah, Ghazi (2001) 'Guest Commentary: Intifadat al-Aqsa and the Bloody Road to Palestinian Independence', *Political Geography* 20(2), 135–137.

Fine, Robert and Philip Spencer (2017) *Antisemitism and the left: On the return of the Jewish question*, Manchester University Press: Manchester.

Finkelstein, Norman (2002) 'An Introduction to the Israel-Palestine Conflict', *Global Dialogue* 4(3), 1–17.

Fromm, Erich (1964) *The Heart of Man: Its Genius for Good and Evil*, Harper & Row: London.

Fromm, Erich (1956) *The Sane Society*, Routledge: London.

Gallagher, Nancy Elizabeth (1996) *Approaches to the History of the Middle East: Interviews with Leading Middle East Historians*, Ithaca Press: Lebanon.

Golan, Arnon (2001) 'European Imperialism and the Development of Modern Palestine: Was Zionism a Form of Colonialism?', *Space and Polity* 5(2), 127–143.

Gordon, Neve and Moriel Ram (2016) 'Ethnic cleansing and the formation of settler colonial geographies', *Political Geography* 53, 20–29.

Graham, Stephen (2002) 'Bulldozers and Bombs: The Latest Palestinian-Israeli Conflict as Asymmetric Urbicide', *Antipode* 34(4), 642–649.

Gregory, Derek (2004a) *The Colonial Present: Afghanistan, Palestine, Iraq*, Blackwell: Oxford.

Gregory, Derek (2004b) 'Palestine Under Siege', *Antipode* 36(4), 601–606.

Hage, Ghassan (2003) '"Comes a Time We Are All Enthusiasm": Understanding Palestinian Suicide Bombers in Times of Exighophobia', *Public Culture* 15(1), 65–89.

Hassan, Salah (2001) 'Terminus Nation-State: Palestine and the Critique of Nationalism', *New Formations* 45, 54–71.

Hussein, Cherine (2015) 'The single-state alternative in Palestine/Israel', *Conflict, Security & Development* 15(5), 521–547.

Hussein, Cherine (2014) 'Palestine, Israel and the one-state solution: an interview with Ilan Pappé', *Critical Studies on Terrorism* 7(3), 484–493.

Jamoul, Lina (2004) 'Palestine – In Search of Dignity', *Antipode* 36 (4), 581–595.

Judt, Tony (2003) 'Israel: The Alternative', *The New York Review*, https://www.nybooks.com/articles/2003/10/23/israel-the-alternative/, last accessed 9 March 2022.

Katz, Cindi and Neil Smith (2003) 'An interview with Edward Said', *Environment and Planning D: Society and Space* 21, 635–651.

Khalidi, Walid (2003) 'The Prospects of Peace in the Middle East', *Journal of Palestine Studies* 32(2), 50–62.

Kramer, Martin (2001) *Ivory Towers on Sand: The Failure of Middle Eastern Studies in America*, The Washington Institute for Near East Policy: Washington DC.

Lustick, Ian (2021) 'On Palestine-Israel One-State Reality', Vimeo, https://vimeo.com/530036446, last accessed 11 March 2022.

Lustick, Ian (2019) *Paradigm Lost: From Two-State Solution to One-State Reality*, University of Pennsylvania Press: Philadelphia.

Mahmood, Syed, Emily Wroe, Arlan Fuller and Jennifer Leaning (2016) 'The Rohingya people of Myanmar: health, human rights, and identity', *Lancet* 389(10081), 1841–1850.

Mansour, Camille (2001) 'Israel's Colonial Impasse', *Journal of Palestine Studies* 30(4), 83–87.

Munson, Henry (1996) 'Intolerable Tolerance: Western Academia and Islamic Fundamentalism', *Contention* 5, 99–117.

Pappé, Ilan (2013) 'Revisiting 1967: The false paradigm of peace, partition and parity', *Settler Colonial Studies* 3(3–4), 341–351.

Pappé, Ilan (2007) '"Two States or One State": A debate between former Knesset Member Uri Avnery and Doctor Ilan Pappé', *The Saker*, http://thesaker.is/two-states-or-one-state-a-debate-between-avnery-and-pappe/, last accessed 8 March 2022.

Pappé, Ilan (2006) 'The 1948 Ethnic Cleansing of Palestine', *Journal of Palestine Studies* 36(1), 6–20.

Piterburg, Gabriel (2001) 'Erasing the Palestinians', *New Left Review* 10, 31–46.

Randall, Daniel (2021) *Confronting Antisemitism on the Left: Arguments for Socialists*, No Pasaran Media: London.

Rodinson, Maxime (1983) *Cult, Ghetto, and State: The Persistence of the Jewish Question*, Al Saqi Books: London.

Rodinson, Maxime (1968) *Israel and the Arabs*, Penguin Books: Middlesex.

Rogers, Alistair, Noel Castree and Rob Kitchen (2013) *Dictionary of Human Geography*, Oxford University Press: Oxford.

Ronayne, Peter (2004) 'Genocide in Kosovo', *Human Rights Review* 5(4), 57–71.

Said, Edward (2001) 'The Desertions of Arafat', *New Left Review* 11, https://newleftreview.org/issues/ii11/articles/edward-said-the-desertions-of-arafat, last accessed 17 March 2022.

Said, Edward (2000) 'America's Last Taboo', *New Left Review* 6, https://newleftreview.org/issues/ii6/articles/edward-said-america-s-last-taboo, last accessed 17 March 2020.

Said, Edward (1999) 'The One-State Solution', *New York Times Magazine*, https://www.nytimes.com/1999/01/10/magazine/the-one-state-solution.html, last accessed 8 March 2022.

Said, Edward (1995) *Orientalism*, Penguin Books: London.

Said, Edward (1986) 'On Palestinian Identity: A Conversation with Salman Rushdie', *New Left Review* 160, 63–80.

Said, Edward (1985) 'An Ideology of Difference', *Critical Inquiry* 12(1), 38–58.

Smith Finley, Joanne (2021) 'Why Scholars and Activists Increasingly Fear a Uyghur Genocide in Xinjiang', *Journal of Genocide Research* 23(3), 348–370.

Taji-Farouki, Suha (2004) 'Thinking on the Jews', in Taji-Farouki, Suha and Basheer M. Nafir (editors) *Islamic Thought in the Twentieth Century*, I.B. Tauris: London, 318–375.

Tilley, Virginia (2005) *The One-State Solution: A Breakthrough for Peace in the Israeli-Palestinian Deadlock*, University of Michigan Press: Ann Arbor.

Todorova, Teodora (2015) 'Reframing Bi-nationalism in Palestine-Israel as a Process of Settler Decolonisation', *Antipode* 47(5), 1367–1387.

Ullah, Ahsan (2016) 'Rohingya Crisis in Myanmar: Seeking Justice for the "Stateless"', *Journal of Contemporary Criminal Justice* 32(3), 285–301.

Veracini, Lorenzo (2019) 'Israel-Palestine Through a Settler-colonial Studies Lens', *Interventions* 21(4), 568–581.

Webman, Esther (2015) 'The "Jew" as a Metaphor for Evil in Arab Public Discourse', *The Journal of the Middle East and Africa* 6(3–4), 275–292.

Wolfe, Patrick (2006) 'Settler colonialism and the elimination of the native', *Journal of Genocide Research* 8(4), 387–409.

Yiftachel, Oren (2002) 'Territory as the Kernel of the Nation: Space, Time and Nationalism in Israel/Palestine', *Geopolitics* 7(2), 215–248.

Chapter 4

Brown, Wendy (1995) *States of Injury: power and freedom in late modernity*, Princeton University Press: Princeton, NJ.

Cesarani, David (2004) *The Left and the Jews: The Jews and the Left*, Labour Friends of Israel: London.

Cohen, Ben (2004) *A Discourse of Delegitimisation: The British Left and the Jews*, https://archive.jpr.org.uk/download?id=2228, last accessed 6 July 2022.

Cohen, Steve (2005) *That's Funny You Don't Look Anti-Semitic*, Engage: London, https://www.workersliberty.org/files/2020-11/thatsfunny.pdf, last accessed 20 September 2022.

Fine, Robert and Philip Spencer (2017) *Antisemitism and the left: On the return of the Jewish question*, Manchester University Press: Manchester.

Golan, Arnon (2001) 'European Imperialism and the Development of Modern Palestine: Was Zionism a Form of Colonialism?', *Space and Polity* 5(2), 127–143.

Lenin, Vladimir (1975) *Questions of National Policy and Proletarian Internationalism*, Progress Publishers: Moscow.

Lenin, Vladimir (1916) 'A Caricature of Marxism and Imperialist Economism', *Marxists Internet Archive*, http://www.marxists.org/archive/lenin/works/1916/carimarx/4.htm, last accessed 6 July 2022.

Lenin, Vladimir (1913) 'Draft Platform for the Fourth Congress of Social-Democrats of the Latvian Area', *Marxists Internet Archive*, http://www.marxists.org/archive/lenin/works/1913/may/31.htm, last accessed 6 July 2022.

Lenin, Vladimir (1903) 'The Position of the Bund in the Party', *Marxists Internet Archive*, http://www.marxists.org/archive/lenin/works/1903/oct/22a.htm, last accessed 6 July 2022.

Marx, Karl (1843) 'On the Jewish Question', in David McLellan (editor) (1977) *Karl Marx: Selected Writings*, Oxford University Press: Oxford, 39–62.

Marx, Karl (1845) 'The Holy Family: The Jewish Question No. 3', *Marxists Internet Archive*, https://www.marxists.org/archive/marx/works/1845/holy-family/ch06_3_b.htm, last accessed 6 July 2022.

McLellan, David (1980) *Marx before Marxism*, Papermac Macmillan: Basingstoke.

Nir, Oded and Joel Wainwright (2018) 'Where Is the Marxist Critique of Israel/Palestine?', *Rethinking Marxism* 30(3), 336–355.

Rapoport, Louis (1990) *Stalin's War Against the Jews: The Doctors' Plot and the Soviet Solution*, The Free Press: New York.

Rodinson, Maxime (1983) *Cult, Ghetto, and State: The Persistence of the Jewish Question*, Al Saqi Books: London.

Rodinson, Maxime (1973) *Israel: A Colonial-Settler State?*, Pathfinder: London.

Rodinson, Maxime (1968) *Israel and the Arabs*, Penguin Books: Middlesex.

Trotsky, Leon (2007) 'Trotsky on the national question', *Workers Liberty*, https://www.workersliberty.org/story/2017-07-26/trotsky-national-question, last accessed 6 July 2022.

Trotsky, Leon (1970) *On the Jewish Question*, Pathfinder Press: New York.

Trotsky, Leon (1939) 'Independence of the Ukraine and Sectarian Muddleheads', *Marxists Internet Archive*, http://www.marxists.org/archive/trotsky/1939/07/ukraine.htm, last accessed 6 July 2022.

Tuck, Eve and K. Wayne Yang (2012) 'Decolonization is not a metaphor', *Decolonization: Indigeneity, Education & Society* 1(1), 1–40.

Vaksberg, Arkady (1994) *Stalin Against the Jews*, Alfred A. Knopf Inc: New York.

Wistrich, Robert (editor) (1979) *The Left Against Zion: Communism, Israel and the Middle East*, Vallentine, Mitchell and Co.: London.

Wolfe, Patrick (2012) 'New Jews for old: Settler state formation and the impossibility of Zionism: In memory of Edward W. Said', *Arena* 37/38, 285–321.

Chapter 5

BBC (2016) 'Labour suspends activist over alleged anti-Semitic comments', BBC News, https://www.bbc.co.uk/news/uk-england-kent-36203911, last accessed 14 November 2022.

Berg, Marita (2013) '"Degenerate" Music', DW, https://www.dw.com/en/the-nazis-take-on-degenerate-music/a-16834697, last accessed 27 July 2022.

Fine, Robert and Philip Spencer (2017) *Antisemitism and the left: On the return of the Jewish question*, Manchester University Press: Manchester.

Gates, Henry Louis Jr. (2020) 'How Societies Go Backward', *The New York Review*, https://www.nybooks.com/articles/2020/11/19/how-societies-go-backward/, last accessed 25 July 2020.

Gates, Henry Louis Jr. (1994) 'The Uses of Anti-Semitism, with Memoirs of an Anti-Anti-Semite', in Paul Berman (editor) *Blacks and Jews: Alliances and Arguments*, Dell Publishing: New York, 217–228.

Gilroy, Paul (2000) *Against Race: Imagining Political Culture beyond the Color Line*, The Belknap Press of Harvard University: Cambridge, Massachusetts.

Mosse, George L. (1985) *Toward the Final Solution: A History of European Racism*, The University of Wisconsin Press: Wisconsin.

West, Cornel (2007) *Voices on Antisemitism*, United States Holocaust

Memorial Museum, https://www.ushmm.org/antisemitism/podcast/voices-on-antisemitism/cornel-west, last accessed 25 July 2022.

West, Cornel (1994) 'On Black-Jewish Relations', in Paul Berman (editor) *Blacks and Jews: Alliances and Arguments*, Dell Publishing: New York, 144–153.

Chapter 6

Arendt, Hannah (1976) *The Origins of Totalitarianism*, A Harvest Book: London.

Ashe, Stephen D. and Brendan McGeever (2011) 'Marxism, racism and the construction of "race" as a social and political relation: an interview with Professor Robert Miles', *Ethnic and Racial Studies* 34(12), 2009–2026.

Fine, Robert and Philip Spencer (2017) *Antisemitism and the left: On the return of the Jewish question*, Manchester University Press: Manchester.

Miles, Robert (1993) *Racism after 'race relations'*, Routledge: London.

INDEX

academic freedom 27
aesthetics 51, 55
African Link, The (Barker) 37
agency, human 12, 88
Ahasverus, myth of 57, 59
al-Afghani, Jamal ad-din 106
Algeria 72, 115
Anglo-Saxon 'race' 55
anti-Arab racism *see* anti-Muslim racism, Islamophobia, and Orientalism
anti-black racism 43, 51–2, 53, 54, 78, 140–1, 148, *149*; *see also* colonial model of racism
anti-Jewish racism; *see also* anti-Zionism
  aesthetics 55
  black antisemitism 140–7
  in colonial model of racism 37–9, 45–6, 65
  compared with Islamophobia 62–4
  excluded from academic research 31, 36
  First World War's impact on 58–9
  history of 48–9
  Islamist 91–3, 119
  Jews seen as threat 20, 31, 45–6, 53, 56–7, 58–60, 61–4, 84, 102, 113, 144
  Klug's 'antisemitism' definition 8, 14
  the Left's 156–7; *see also* 'Jewish question, the'
    blind spot 17–18, 153
    defence against 8
    demanding exceptionalism 1–2, 11, 12–14, 15–16
    Finkelstein's trivialising of 20–2
    'the harmful Jew' *see* 'Jewish question, the'
    litmus test 18–20
    Randall's three strands 75
    refusal to see/acknowledge 2, 14–15
  linguistics 52, 53
  of Nazi Germany 148, *149*

Rodinson's views 118–19
weaponised by Zionists 13, 15–16, 24, 37, 101–2, 118
anti-Judaism 48–9
anti-Muslim racism 7–8, 38, 48, 49, 62–4, 83, 87; *see also* Islamophobia and Orientalism
anti-whitism 142
anti-Zionism; *see also* Zionism
academic boycott of Israel 18–19
of the Arab world 119
calls to dismantle Israel 2, 20, 84, 85, 92, 93–6, 113
claim of 'not racism' 12–14, 17–18, 19, 21–6, 101–2
Daphne's story 14–16
as racism 157–8
Rodinson's views 111–13, 117–19, 122
Stalinist 75
'Anti-Zionism is not antisemitism' meeting (SWP) 22–4
antisemitism *see* anti-Jewish racism
Antisemitism and the left (Fine and Spencer)
'the Jewish question' 8, 9, 69, 101, 103, 139
on Marx 124, 134
'othering' of Jews 96
Palestinian-Israeli conflict 31, 71, 96
racism vs. universalism 69
'real humanism' 134
apartheid 78–9, 81

Arab–Israeli war (1967) 65, 72, 84
Arab world; *see also* Palestinian-Israeli conflict
anti-Jewish racism and anti-Zionism 91–3, 110–11, 119
nationalism 104, 106–7
racism against 7–8, 38, 48, 49, 62–4, 83, 87
rejection of UN partition plan 109
resentment of European colonialism 107, 109
Arendt, Hannah 1, 153–4
Aryan 'race' myth 52–3, 54

Back, Les 31
Balfour Declaration (1917) 107, 109
Barker, Anthony J. 37
Bashir, Bashir 94
Bauer, Bruno 124–7, 135
Bauer, Otto 128
Bauman, Zygmunt 49, 59–60, 60–1
Ben Gurion, David 108, 109
'Between Pariah and Parvenu' (Arendt) 153–4
Biltmore Program (1942) 108
biophilia 90–1
black antisemitism 140–8
black people, racism against *see* anti-black racism
Black Power (Carmichael and Hamilton) 34
Blauner, Robert 34, 42–3

Bosnia and Herzegovina 44
Boycott, Divestment and Sanctions movement 19, 78, 79
Bradley, Michael 144
Brah, Avtar 10
Brown, Malcolm *see Racism* (Miles and Brown)
Brown, Wendy 12, 121, 122
'Building the Campaign for Free Speech' conference 25–6
Busbridge, Rachel 77–8, 94–5, 96

Cadman, Louisa 12
capitalism
  and anti-Zionism 64, 110, 113, 117
  and antisemitism 54–5, 58, 60–1, 62, 75, 113, 133–4
  identity politics 12, 121, 125
  and nationalism 130–2
  and racism 35–6, 37, 39–46; *see also* colonial model of racism
Carmichael, Stokely 34
'chain of being' notion 51
China 16–17, 78
Christianity 47–9, 50, 57–8, 143
civilisation 41–2, 49
co-dependency 139–40
Cohen, Philip 61, 62
Cohen, Steve 123
colonial model of racism; *see also* Palestinian-Israeli conflict, in Left's thinking; settler-colonialism
  and capitalism 33, 35–6, 43–4
  European superiority 49–50, 105
  implications for antisemitism and Zionism 37–8
  Orientalism 70–1
  reification of 'race' 42, 43, 44–5
  settler-colonialism *see* settler-colonialism
  in the UK 34–5
  in the US 34
  'white-over-black' relationship 32, 33–4, 35, 42–3, 65, 77, 78, 83–4
'"Comes a Time We Are All Enthusiasm"' (Hage) 87
common-sense ideology 39–40, 60, 156
Confronting Antisemitism on the Left (Randall) 75
contradictory consciousness 39–40
Corbyn, Jeremy 22–3, 24–5
Cousin, Glynis 31
Cuba 72

Dalsheim, Joyce 85–6
Daphne (Jewish anti-Zionist) 15–16
de Lapouge, Comte Georges Vacher 54
'Decolonization is not a metaphor' (Tuck and Yang) 120
democracy, consistent 123–4, 130–2, 135
democracy, socialist 121

INDEX

Drumont, Edouard 58
dual camp politics 35, 75

emancipation 69, 121, 123–7, 134–5, 139–40, 153–4; *see also* freedom
Engels, Frederick 11–12
Entartete Musik exhibition (Nazis) 148, *149*
environmental determinism 47, 50
Essay on the Inequality of Human Races, 1853– 55 (Gobineau) 54
essentialism 10–11, 12, 44, 64, 140, 147
ethnic cleansing 44, 79–86
eugenics 55
exceptionalising
    Israel 15, 19, 79, 84, 97, 102, 117, 135, 154–5
    Jews 1, 2, 9, 11, 13, 15–16, 18, 154–5

Faisal I 106
Falah, Ghazi 74, 81, 83–4, 87
Farrakhan, Louis 141, 142
fascism 34, 42–3, 82–3, 84, 107–8
Fine, Robert *see Antisemitism and the left* (Fine and Spencer)
Finkelstein, Norman 20–2, 27, 81
First World War 58–9, 107
Formby, Jennie 24–5
France 41, 104, 107

freedom 53, 122, 126, 147; *see also* emancipation
Fromm, Erich 90–1

Galton, Francis 55
Gates, Henry Louis, Jr. 140, 141, 144–7, 148
genocide 42–3, 79–80, 81, 82, 96, 97, 156, 157; *see also* Holocaust
German National Socialist (Nazi) party 42–3, 45, 56, 58, 59, 82–3, 107–8, 148, *149*; *see also* Holocaust
Ghanem, As'ad 18–19
Gilroy, Paul 8–9, 36, 139
Gobineau, Arthur de 53, 54
Golan, Arnon 72
Gordon, Neve 12–13, 79–80
Graham, Stephen 81–2, 89
Gramsci, Antonio 39–40
Gregory, Derek 82, 83–4, 87
Guardian 18
Guillemin, Colette 45

Hage, Ghassan 87, 88–9, 90, 91, 95
Hall, Stuart 36
Hamas 86, 87, 93
Hamilton, Charles 34
Herzl, Theodor 105
history, defining 11–12
history of modern racism 50–60
Hitler, Adolf 59, 82; *see also* German National Socialist (Nazi) party

Holocaust 36, 42–3, 60, 80, 82–3, 97, 107–8, 108–9, 118–19, 143, 156
Holy Family (Marx) 124–5, 127
humanism 134–5
Hussein, Cherine 78, 94, 96

Iceman Inheritance, The (Bradley) 144
identity politics 10–11, 12, 121–2, 140, 155–6
ideology, racism as 7, 31, 32–3, 34, 39–46, 54, 60, 155, 156
immigration 39, 42, 56, 107, 108
imperialism 64, 65, 72, 75, 105–7, 108–9, 110–11, 117, 132; *see also* colonial model of racism
incommensurability, ethic of 120–1, 143
'In Defence of Free Speech' meeting (2020) 24–5
India 1–2, 7, 52, 158
Ireland 114
Islam *see* Arab world
Islamophobia 7–8, 48, 62–4, 83; *see also* anti-Muslim racism and Orientalism
Israel; *see also* anti-Zionism; Palestinian-Israeli conflict; Zionism
   1948 declaration of state of 109
   academic boycott of 18–20
   Arab–Israeli war (1967) 65, 72, 73
   calls to dismantle 2, 20, 70, 84, 85, 92, 93–6, 153, 155
   colonial origins of 104–10
   criticism of 12, 13, 17–19, 84, 101–2; *see also* anti-Zionism
   exceptionalising 15, 19, 79, 84, 97, 102, 117, 135, 154–5
   Islamist view of 92–3
   legal foundations 83
   nationalism *see* Zionism
   as *the* Other 70, 156
   political limitations 111
   Right, rise of the 24, 141
   right to exist 115, 116
   as settler-colonialism 32, 33, 71, 77–9, 83–4, 112–14
   'South-Africanising' 78–9
   territorial expansion 65, 80, 85, 92
   as threat 62, 83–4, 95, 101, 113, 155
   United States, relations with the 83
   weaponising antisemitism 13, 15–16, 22–7, 37–9, 101–2, 118

Jamoul, Lina 84, 85, 89–90
Jeffries, Leonard 141, 142
'Jewish question, the'; *see also* anti-Jewish racism and anti-Zionism
   calls to dismantle Israel 84, 85, 95–6, 102, 113
   defining 3, 8

INDEX

distortion of universalism 69, 85–6, 139
exceptionalism 15–16, 84, 102
Jews as threat 20, 22, 31, 102
Marxist views 123–34
and Muslim-Jewish relationship 91–2
political problem 154–5
Jewish Question, The (Bauer) 124–5
Jewry's Victory over Teutonism (Marr) 57
Jews
  anti-Zionists 13, 15–16
  the Bund 127–8, 129–31
  exceptionalising 1, 2, 9, 11, 13, 15–16, 18, 154–5
  humanity 134
  as 'immoral capitalists' 54–5, 57–8, 60–1, 145–6
  nationalism 127–8, 129–31, 133–4; *see also* Zionism
  as Other 45–6, 48–9, 59, 61–2, 64, 70, 96, 144
  as persecuted-turned-persecutors 80, 82–4
  racialisation of 8, 12–14, 45, 55–6, 58, 62–4, 69–70, 77, 84–5, 153–6
  racism against *see* anti-Jewish racism
  as threat *see* 'Jewish question, the'
  as ultra-white and uber-privileged 153
  'wandering Jew' 57, 59, 61–2
  Yiddish language 53, 127, 133
Johnson-Lodge Immigration Act (1924) (US) 42
'Jonny' image 148, *149*
Judt, Tony 76, 95

Keddie, Nikki 73–4
Kenya 43–4
Kerensky, Alexander 107
Khalidi, Walid 87, 88
Klug, Brian 8, 14–16
Knox, Robert 55
Kramer, Martin 73

Labour party (UK) 15–16, 22–3, 24–7
'Lawrence of academia syndrome' 91
League of Nations 107
Lenin, Vladimir 123, 128–32, 135
linguistics 45, 52, 53
Livingstone, Ken 15
Lustick, Ian 77

McLellan, David 124
Mansour, Camille 76
Marr, Wilheim 57
Marx, Karl 11, 121, 123–7, 134, 135
Massad, Joseph 87
Mein Kampf (Hitler) 82
Miles, Robert
  anti-Jewish racism 37, 42–3, 46, 48–9, 56, 59

colonial model of racism 31–2, 34–6, 37, 42–3, 43–4
ethnic cleansing 44
Islamophobia 63–4
prehistory of 'race' 46–50
'race,' reification of 10–11, 33, 36, 44, 155–6
racialised identities 155
racism and nationalism 52–3, 54, 55
racism as common-sense ideology 39, 60
Self vs. Other 40–1, 46, 64
Miller, David 17, 20, 24–7
Modernity and the Holocaust (Bauman) 59–60
monstra 47
Mosse, George
anti-Jewish racism 45, 53, 54, 55, 57–8, 59
'Jonny' image 148
'racial' science 50–2, 53, 54, 56–7
racism and nationalism 52, 54
Muslim world *see* Arab world
Myanmar 78

national cultural autonomy (NCA) 128–32
nationalism 33, 52–6, 59–60, 104, 127–33, 135, 140, 141, 143, 146–7; *see also* Zionism
Nazis *see* German National Socialist (Nazi) party
necrophilia 90–1

Netanyahu, Benjamin 23–4
Neumann, Michael 88–9
'"New Anti-Semitism," The' (Gordon) 12–13
New Left Review 72
Nommo newspaper (UCLA) 144
North Vietnam 72
Norway 131–2

On the Jewish Question (Marx) 121, 123–7
'On Black-Jewish Relations' (West) 141–3
Orientalism 38, 70–1, 73–5, 83, 86–7, 91
Orientalism (Said) 37, 38, 65, 70–1, 73–5
Oslo Accords 75–6
Othering
colonial model of racism 43–4
of global East 71
history of 46–50
of Jews 45–6, 48–9, 59, 61–2, 64, 144
by Nazis 148, *149*
outside of Europe 64
Self vs. Other 7–8, 32–3, 40–1
in settler-versus-native dichotomy 121
of Zionists 11, 12, 13, 20, 70, 140, 156
Ottoman Empire 48, 104, 107

Pakistan 158

INDEX

Palestine, British Mandate over 107
Palestinian-Israeli conflict
  1948 war 69, 76, 81, 84, 109, 116, 132
  1967 war 65, 72, 73, 84
  consistent democracy approach 132
  Islamist view of 92–3
  Islamophobia and antisemitism 62
  in Left's thinking
    dissolution solution 20, 84, 85
    ethic of incommensurability 120–1, 143
    ethnic cleansing and genocide 79–86
    'the harmful Jew' 11
    identity politics 140, 156
    Jews as persecuted-turned-persecutors 82–4
    one-state solution 75–7
    Palestinian suicide bombers 86–93
    pro-Palestinian/anti-Israeli 69–70, 72–3, 75
    Said's impact 73–4, 75
    settler-colonialism 32, 38–9, 71, 75–9, 85–6, 96–7, 120–1
    'South-Africanising' 78
    temporal freeze 11, 85
Palestine Liberation Organisation's charter 72–3
racialisation 74, 77, 83, 85–6, 96, 97, 122, 140, 156
resolutions
  dissolution of Israel 20, 84, 85, 93–6
  one-state 75–7, 93–6
  Rodinson's ideas 110–16
  'two nations, two states' 116, 132
Rodinson's history of 110–13
suicide bombers 11, 86–93, 97, 119
Pappé, Ilan 20, 22–4, 27, 69, 77, 78, 81, 88, 93
Piterberg, Gabriel 80–1
Political Geography 18–19
Portraits of White Racism (Wellman) 34
postcolonialism 70–1; *see also* settler-colonialism
Protocols of the Elders of Zion 58, 92, 144
Proudhon, Pierre-Joseph 58

Qutb, Sayyid 91–2

'Race ends here' (Gilroy) 36
'race,' idea of
  colonial model of racism *see* colonial model of racism
  common-sense ideology 39, 60
  dangers of 8–9, 40–1
  history of 46–50
  reification of 33, 36, 42, 43, 44, 45

'race relations' 35–6, 42, 43
Races of Man (Knox) 55
'racial' classification 45, 51, 52–3
Racial Oppression in America (Blauner) 34
'racial' science 46, 50–3, 54, 56–7, 60
'racial' souls 51
racialisation 7–8, 12–13, 32–3, 40–1, 63–4
raciology 8–9
racism; *see also* Othering
 anti-Jewish *see* anti-Jewish racism
 and capitalism 35–6, 37, 39–46; *see also* colonial model of racism
 claim that anti-Zionism is not 12–14, 17–18, 19, 21–6, 101–2
 colonial model *see* colonial model of racism
 conceptualising 39–46
 defining 7
 history of modern 50–60
 history, pre-modern 46–50
 idea of 'race' *see* 'race,' idea of
 as ideology 7, 31, 32–3, 34, 39–46, 54, 60, 155, 156
 and nationalism 33, 52–6, 59–60, 140, 141, 143, 146–7; *see also* anti-Zionism
 'race relations' 35–6, 42, 43
 'racial' classification 45, 51, 52–3
 'racial' science 46, 50–3, 54, 56–7, 60
 'racial' souls 51
 racialisation 7–8, 12–13, 32–3, 40–1, 63–4
 raciology 8–9
 and social class 40–2, 43–4
 social construction 7, 8, 10, 44–5, 148, 156–7
Racism (Miles and Brown)
 anti-Jewish racism 59
 colonial model of racism 34–6, 37, 42, 43–4
 ethnic cleansing 44
 Islamophobia 63–4
 prehistory of 'race' 46–50
 racism and nationalism 52–3, 54
 racism as common-sense ideology 39, 60
 Self vs. Other 40–1, 64
Ram, Moriel 79–80
Randall, Daniel 75
Rapoport, Louis 123
religion 47–8, 50–1, 57, 124–7
ressentiment 121–2
Right, the 10, 61
Rodinson, Maxime
 anti-Zionism and antisemitism 116–20
 background 103
 colonial origins of Israel 104–10
 decolonisation 120–2
 humanism 135

INDEX

Orientalism (Said) 71, 74, 75
   resolution of Palestinian-Israeli conflict 110–16
Rosenhead, Jonathan 16
Russia 105, 106, 107, 127–8

Said, Edward 37, 38, 65, 70–1, 73–5, 76, 83
Secret Relationship Between Blacks and Jews, The (Nation of Islam) 145–6
Serbia 81
settler-colonialism 43, 70–1, 75–9, 85–6, 95, 96–7, 110, 114, 120–1
Sivanandan, Ambalavaner 36
Slater, David 18–19
slavery 32, 37, 43–4, 128, 145–6
social classes 41–2, 47, 102, 125, 156
Social Darwinism 55
Socialist Workers' Party (SWP) 14–16, 22, 157–8
Sodhi, Balbir Singh 7–8
Solomos, John 31
South Africa 77, 78, 115
Spencer, Philip *see Antisemitism and the left* (Fine and Spencer)
States of Injury (Brown) 121
Storey, David 19
Sweden 131–2

Taji-Farouki, Suha 91–3
Theories of Race and Racism (Back and Solomos) 31

Thomas, James 63
Tilley, Virginia 76–7, 94
Todorova, Teodora 94
Toussenel, Alphonso 58
Traces of History (Wolfe) 37–8
Trotsky, Leon 123, 128, 132–4, 135
Tuck, Eve 120

Union of Jewish Students 17
United Nations (UN) 78, 109
United States 7–8, 19, 34–5, 42, 72, 83, 111, 128, 140–7
universalism 69, 123–34, 134–5, 147, 159
University and Colleges Union (UCU) 17–18
university, decolonising the 120–2
'Uses of Anti-Semitism, The' (Gates) 144–7

Veracini, Lorenzo 79, 95, 96

Waterman, Stanley 19–20
Wellman, David 34
Werbner, Pnina 62–3
West, Cornel 140–3
White Paper (1939) (UK) 108
Wistrich, Robert 123
Wolfe, Patrick 37–8, 43, 80

Yang, K. Wayne 120
Yiddish language 53, 127, 133
Yiftachel, Oren 18–19, 81
Yugoslavia 79

Zia-Ebrahimi, Reza 64
Ziegler, Hans Severus 148
Zionism; *see also* anti-Zionism; Israel
    Arab world views of 107, 110–11
    Balfour Declaration's impact 107
    British politics, impact of 107, 108–9
    in colonial model of racism 32, 33, 37–9, 65, 71, 75–9, 81, 95, 105–6, 109–10
    comparing to Nazi fascism 82–3, 84
    comparing to South African apartheid 84
    as ethnic cleansing and genocide 79–86
    'hidden hand' accusations 26, 64
    Holocaust's impact 82–3, 107–8, 118–19
    ignoring Palestinians 106, 109
    latecomer or precursor 95–6
    as 'monster' 11, 80–1, 86, 95, 97, 113
    as nationalism 33, 81, 105, 110, 111–12, 127–8, 129–31, 133
    Rodinson's views 111–13, 117–19
    spatial fluidity 84–5
    temporal freeze 84–5
    as war against Left 26
    weaponising antisemitism 13, 15–16, 22–7, 37–9, 101–2, 118
Zionist Organisation 105